26 Interactive Alphabet Mini-Books

Easy-to-make Reproducible Books That Promote Literacy

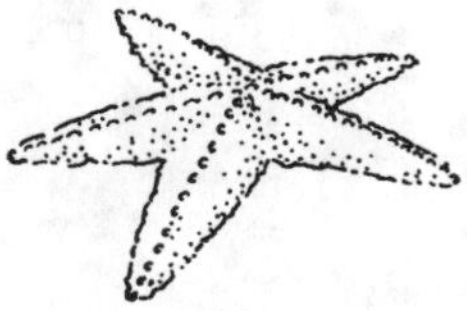

by Mary Beth Spann

SCHOLASTIC
PROFESSIONAL BOOKS

New York • Toronto • London • Auckland • Sydney

Cover design by Vincent Ceci and Jaime Lucero
Cover illustration by James G. Hale

Interior design by Sydney Wright
Interior illustrations by James G. Hale

ISBN 0-590-36506-1

12 11 10 9 8 7 9/9/01/0

Contents

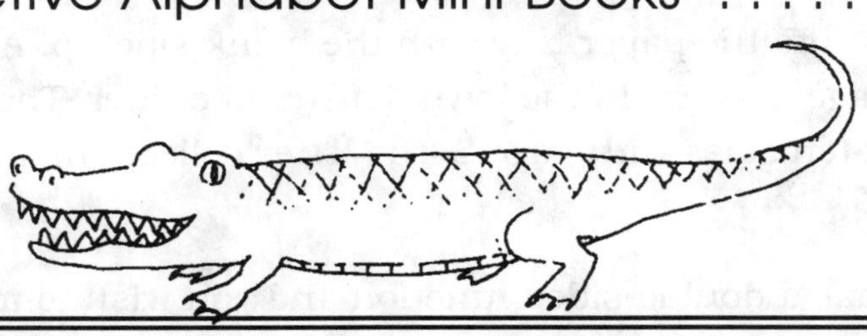

About This Book

26 Interactive Alphabet Mini-Books features a charming collection of reproducible alphabet mini-books that beginning readers will love to make, use, learn from, and collect. There is one mini-book for each letter of the alphabet. They are easy to copy, fold and cut, and equally easy for children to complete and enjoy. The books provide a fun-filled introduction to learning letter sounds and configurations, while inviting children to become acquainted with words beginning with each letter sound. They make a wonderful addition to your existing balanced language arts program as they support your efforts to provide a varied, print-rich classroom environment.

Directions for Printing, Folding, and Cutting Mini-Books

How-to Steps:

1. Make a double-sided copy of the mini-book pages. Start by making a copy of the first page of the mini-book with the title page in the lower left-hand corner of the platen glass.

2. Place this copy into the paper tray with the blank side up. Again, check to be sure that the title page appears in the lower left-hand corner. Then place the second page on the platen glass with page 2 (the letter collection) in the upper left-hand corner.

If your machine has a double-sided function and you wish to make copies that way, you will need to remove the mini-book pages from the book. Regardless of how you make the double-sided copies, you may need to experiment a bit to be sure that the pages are aligned properly and that page 2 appears behind the title page.

3. Cut the page in half along the dotted line.

4. Stack the pages so that page 3 appears behind the title page.

5. Fold the pages in half along the solid line. Once you've checked to be sure that the pages are in the proper order, staple them together along the book's spine.

Ideas for Introducing Alphabet Mini-Books

Begin by providing each child with a copy of the letter book you wish to complete. Read through the book together. Call children's attention to the page numbers featured on each page, and the labeled pictures presented on pages 5-7 in each mini-book. Invite students to color these pictures and the target letter as you complete the book together.

What follows is a page-by-page description of each mini-book followed by an extension activity you may want to try as you and your students complete each page. (Tip: Depending on your class, you may need to assemble the mini-books yourself before presenting them to your students.)

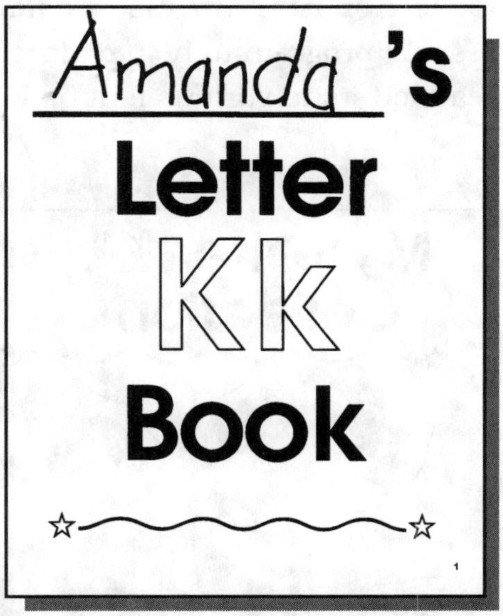

Mini-Book Title Page:

Directions: Each child writes his or her name in the space provided to personalize the book.

Aim: By personalizing each letter book, the child takes "ownership" of the work inside.

Extension Activity: Use a bulletin board to post individual self-portraits or photographs of the children. Each time a student completes a letter book, invite him or her to display it beneath the corresponding picture. Or, post the pictures in a row so as to create a wall border. Then, as each student completes the particular letter book that begins his or her own name, have the students hang their own letter book beneath their picture.

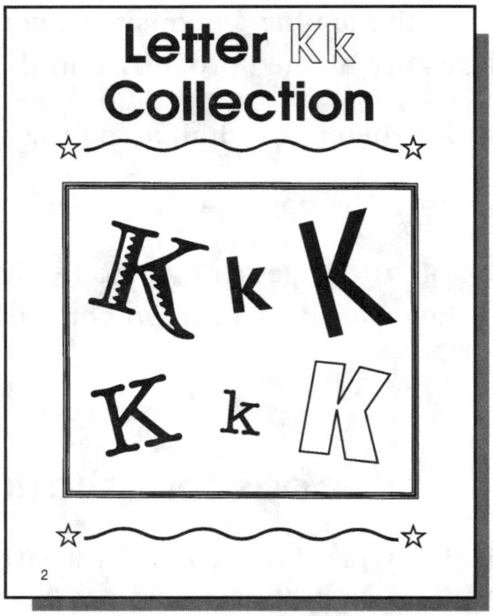

Mini-Book Page 2: Letter Collection

Directions: Children explore the target letter in different fonts.

Aim: To help children realize that letters can be formed in different fonts.

Extension Activity: Use a computer word processing program to help children print out and read letters in various font styles.

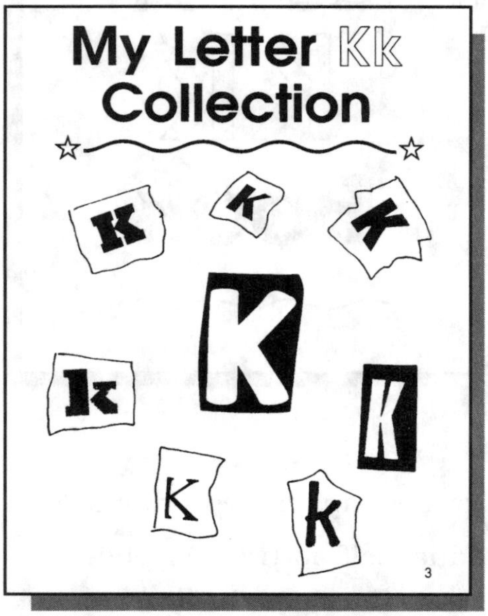

Mini-Book Page 3: My Letter Collection

Directions: Children glue down examples of the target letter clipped or torn from newspapers and magazines.

Aim: To expose children to print as it appears in the world around them, for example on cereal boxes, on neighborhood signs, and in books, magazines, and newspapers.

Extension Activity: Have children create large scale letter collages by clipping individual letters from printed matter and gluing them to oaktag which has been precut into large alphabet letter shapes.

Mini-Book Page 4:

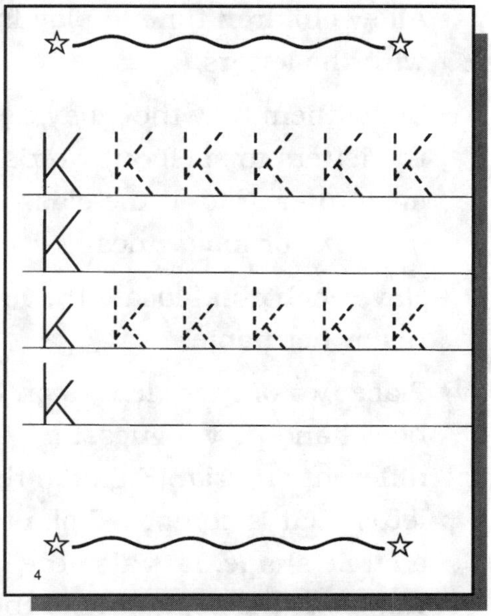

Directions: Children use their fingers then pencils to trace over upper and lowercase outlines of the target letter, then print the same letters on the lines below.

Aim: This page gives children guided printing practice, plus a chance to try printing letters without line constraints.

Extension Activity: Support children's need for tactile learning by having them trace letters in various mediums (finger paint, sand, rice, cereal, etc.). Also, provide bendable materials such as pipe cleaners, clay, and aluminum foil for children to mold into letter shapes.

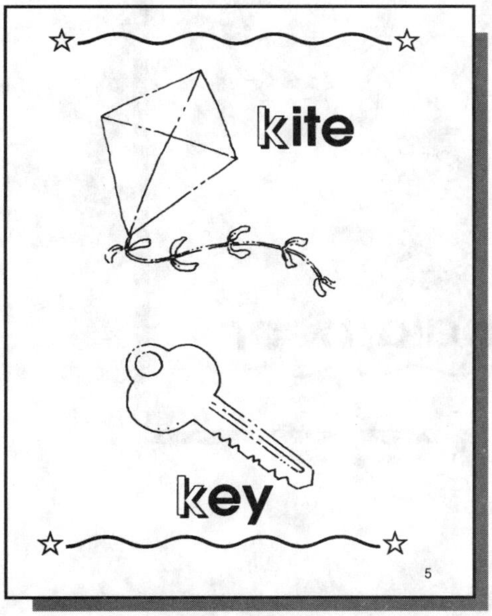

Mini-Book Pages 5, 6, and 7:

Directions: Children identify and color labeled objects that begin with the target letter.

Aim: Children will begin building a vocabulary of words beginning with a particular letter of the alphabet.

Extension Activity: Provide students with a flannel board and alphabet letters cut from assorted pieces of felt. Then try the following:

- Allow children time to play freely with the letters.
- Show them how they may use the letters to spell out words they encounter around the classroom or in books or magazines.
- Have each child locate the first letter of his or her name.
- Place two or more letters on the board and play a guessing game using different criteria. (E.g., I'm thinking of a letter that is composed of a tall stick and a circle shape. It is also the letter that is at the beginning of the word "doll.")
- Have children take turns coming up to the board and closing their eyes. As the class looks on, help the participating child trace the shape of a letter with his or her fingers and then attempt to guess which letter it is.

Mini-Book Page 8:
My Letter Word Bank

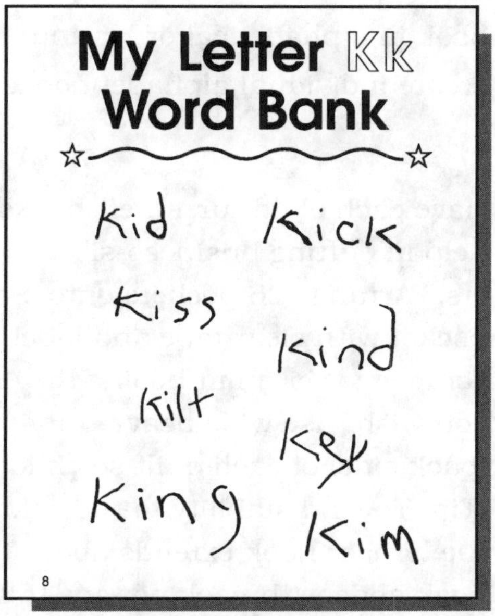

Directions: Children use the space provided to write and/or draw new words beginning with the target letter. They can either write or illustrate the words themselves, or they can cut and paste photos or illustrations of words that begin with the target letter.

Aim: This page encourages children to dip into their own experiences as they choose favorite and familiar words to feature.

Extension Activity: Help children label their illustrations. Also, take time to share children's word collections with the rest of the class. Use chart pad paper to record all the words the class generated for each letter. Consider printing each word onto a separate piece of manila paper and binding these pages into a picture dictionary, with children supplying the illustrations and definitions, if desired.

What to Do With Completed Mini-books

Here are some ideas for getting the most out of your completed mini-books:

Book Rings

Give each child a loose-leaf binder ring on which to collect their books. Store the rings in a box; allow the children to take the rings home after each mini-book addition, or when all the letters books are complete. (Tip: Pipe cleaners bent into circle shapes with the ends twisted together can double as inexpensive "ring" substitutes.)

Mini-Book Masterpieces

Glue each mini-book to the center of a piece of construction paper. Use the border of the construction paper (instead of page 8 of the mini-book) as a Word Bank space to glue or draw and label alphabet pictures. Assemble each child's mounted mini-book in alphabetical order and then bind each set together between oaktag covers to create individual alphabet books for children to treasure.

Alphabet Quilts

Have each child turn their books into an alphabet pocket quilt. Enlist a parent's help in cutting business-size envelopes (saved from junk mail) in half to make "pockets." Arrange 26 pockets onto a piece of oaktag, and glue in place. Reinforce each pocket with clear tape and label them with an alphabet letter. Then, as children complete their mini-books, they may slip each one into its own little paper pocket. If you wish, use wide heavy-duty packing tape to secure a metal hanger to the top (back side) of each quilt so children may hang their creations up in class or at home. (Tip: To lend stability to the oaktag, tape the hanger onto the quilt back so that only the hanger hook extends above the top edge. You may want to wrap sharp hanger hook ends with packing tape to avoid injury.)

Shoe Box Treasure Chests

Ask each student to bring a shoe box to class. Have students create hinged tops for their boxes by taping one of the lid's long sides to the box. If necessary, use a scissors to snip the corners of each box lid apart so that it lifts freely. Cover the boxes and lids with light colored craft paper. Then, have children trace or print alphabet letters onto the paper. Trace the shapes with glue and sprinkle them with glitter. Have students use these boxes as treasure chests for collecting and storing completed mini-books.

Culminating Letter Book Celebration

You may wish to mark the completion of your letter book project by inviting family members in to view the books and celebrate your accomplishment with you. Here are some easy-to-execute ideas to make this party a success:

- Invite children to pick a favorite alphabet mini-book to "read" to the group.
- Prepare other simple alphabet activities to share, such as a rendition of the ABC song, or a walk-through display of related alphabet books, crafts, writing samples and projects.
- Serve alphabet inspired refreshments such as "iced-T", Hi-C™, and homemade cookies cut into letter shapes.

_______'s

Letter Aa Book

A

a

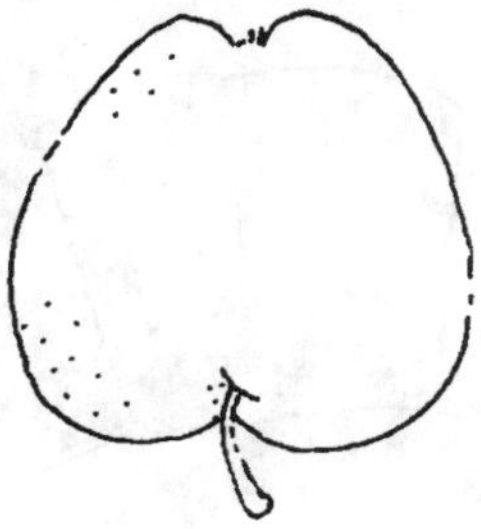

apple

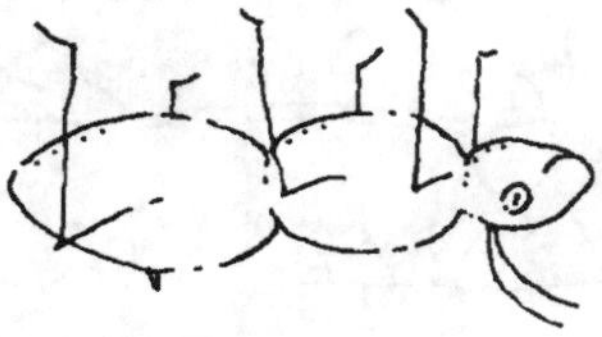

ant

My Letter Aa Word Bank

Letter Aa Collection

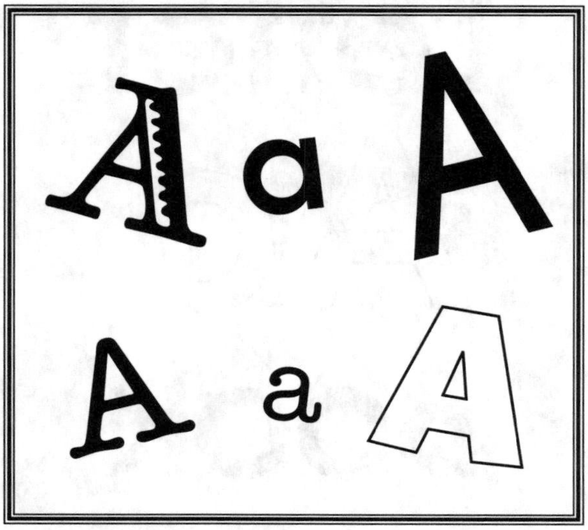

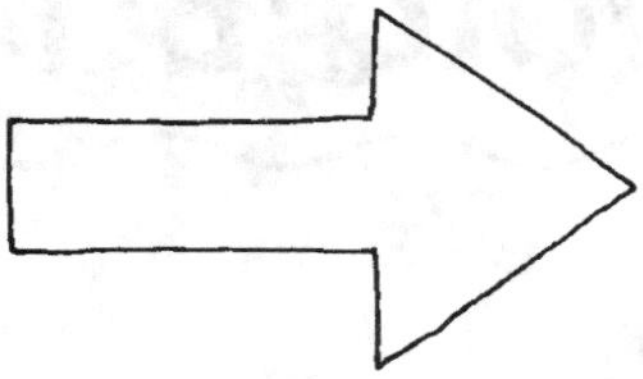

arrow

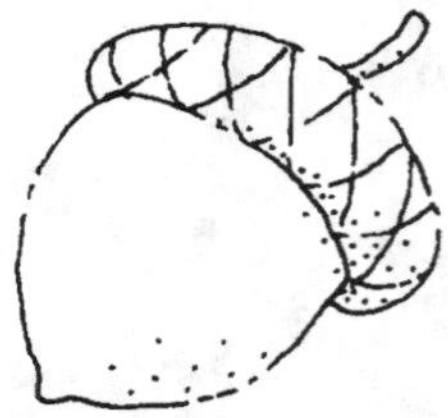

acorn

My Letter Aa Collection

alligator

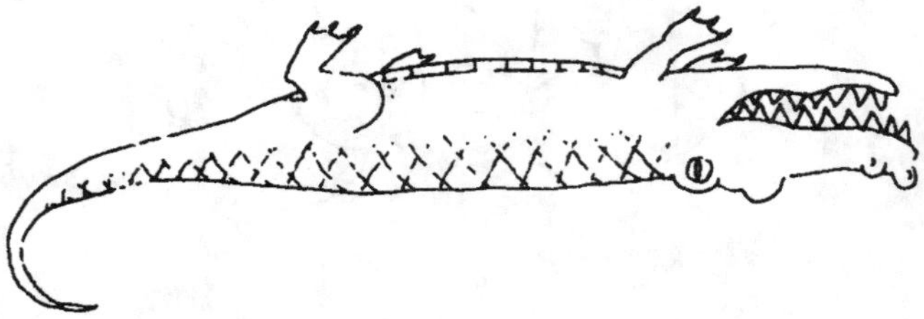

apron

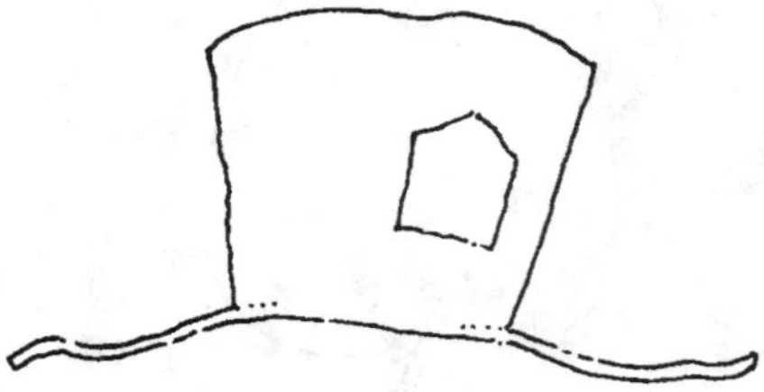

B B B B B B

B

b b b b b b

b

bat

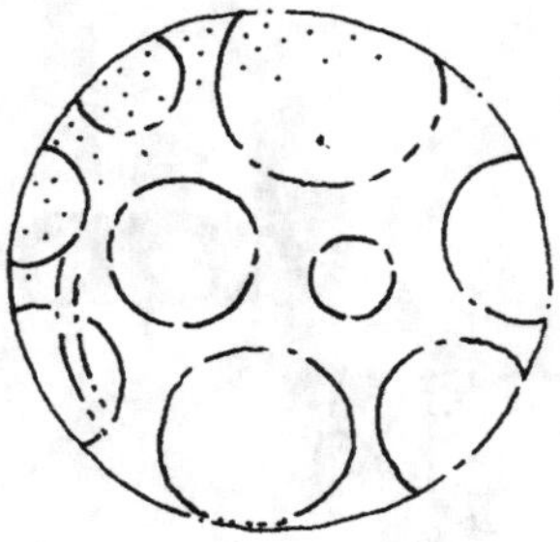

ball

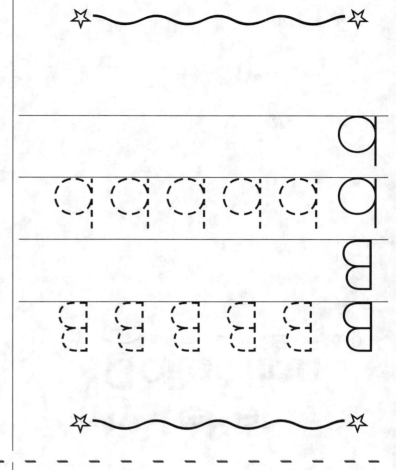

My Letter Bb Word Bank

______________'s

Letter Bb Book

3

My Letter Bb Collection

6

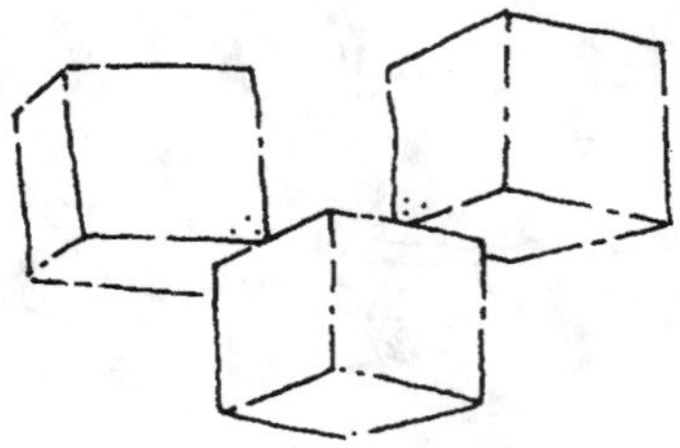

blocks

baby

Letter Bb Collection

B b B

B b B

2

bunny

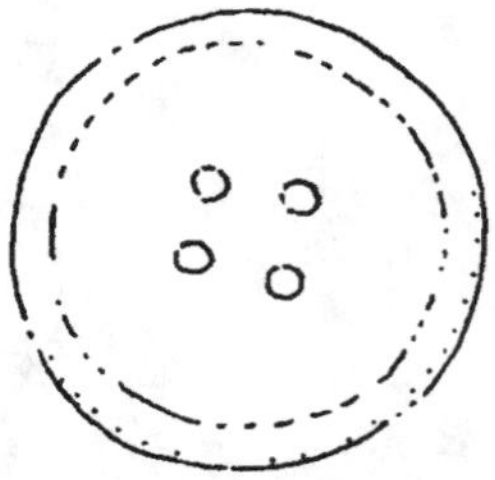

button

7

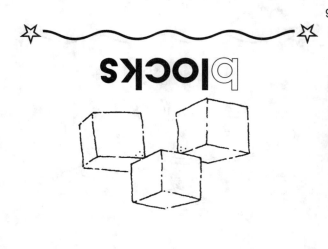

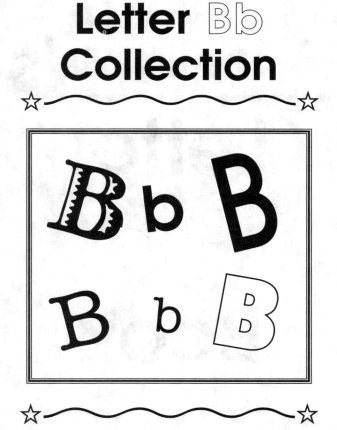

comb

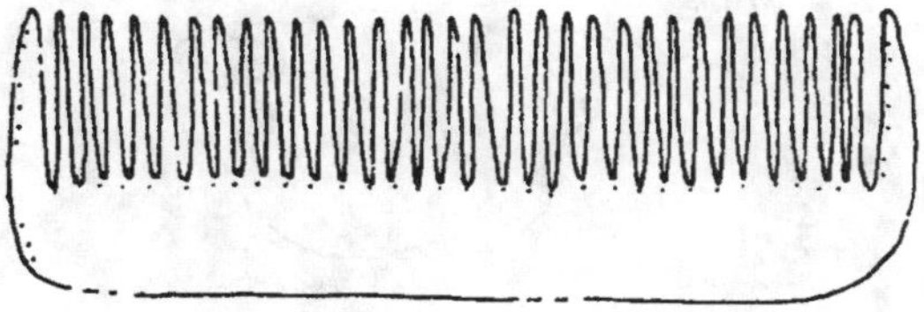

cat

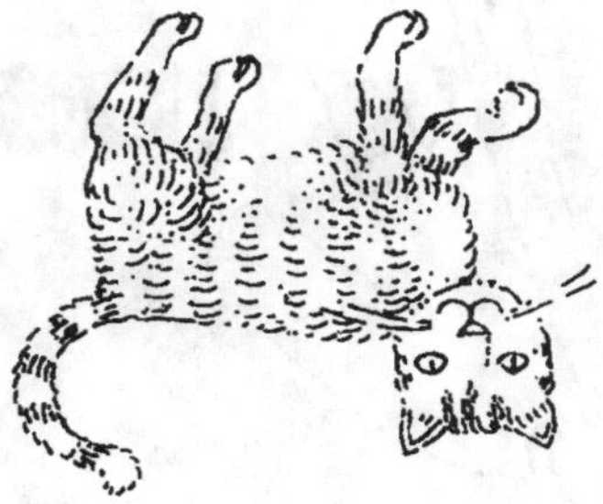

C

C

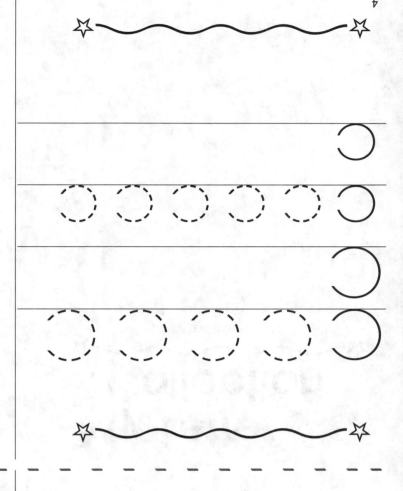

My Letter Cc Word Bank

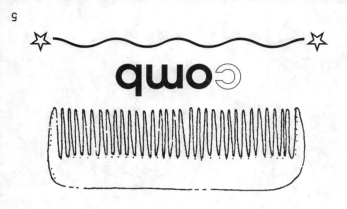

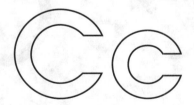

________'s Letter Cc Book

Letter Cc Collection

C c C

C c C

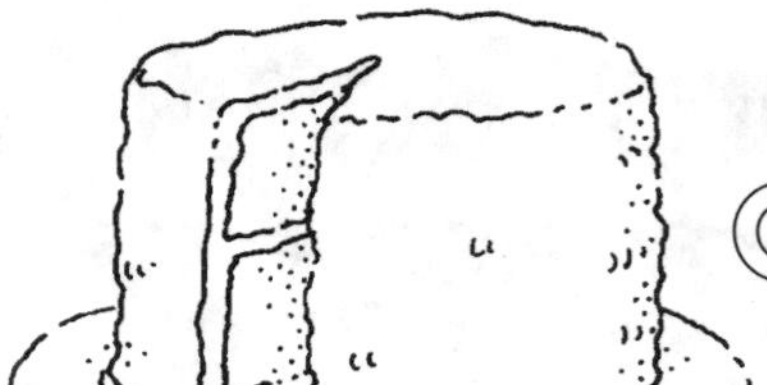

cake

cup

My Letter Cc Collection

cap

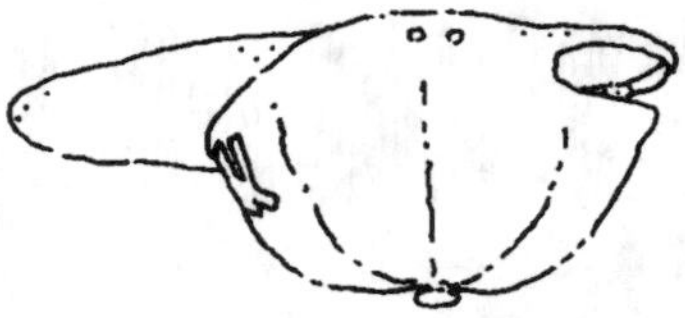

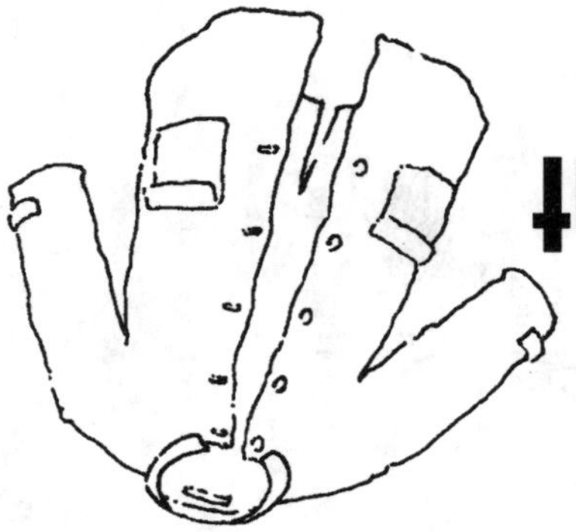

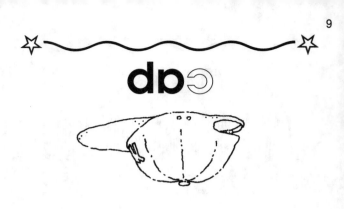

coat

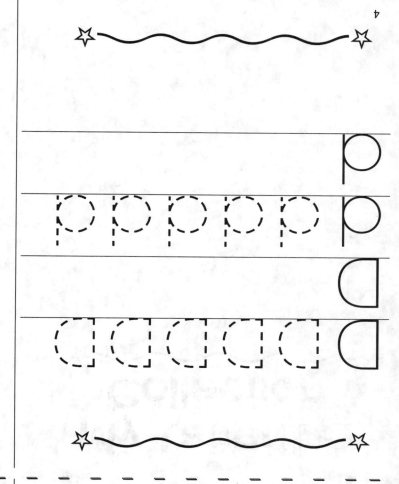

My Letter Dd Word Bank

______'s

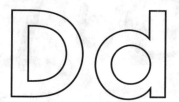

Letter Dd Book

D D D D D D

d d d d d d

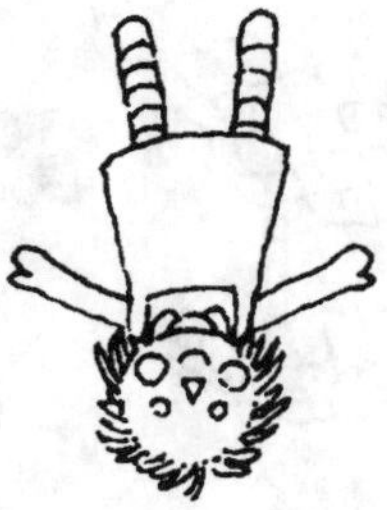

doll

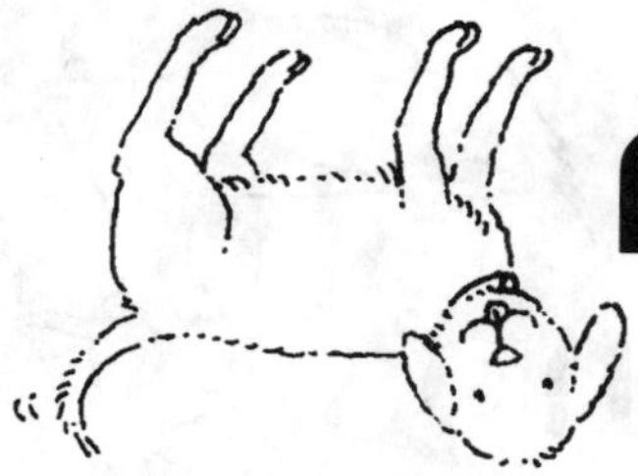

dog

Letter Dd Collection

Dd D

D d D

door

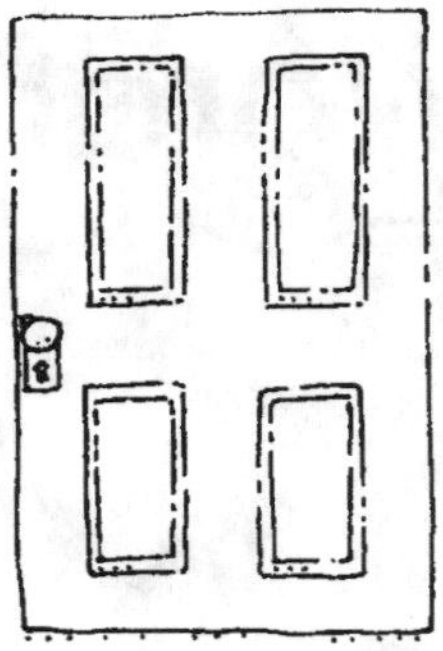

dinosaur

My Letter Dd Collection

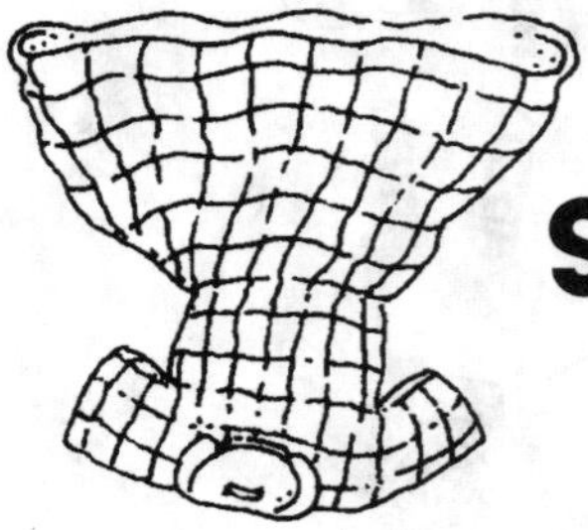

dress

duck

elephant

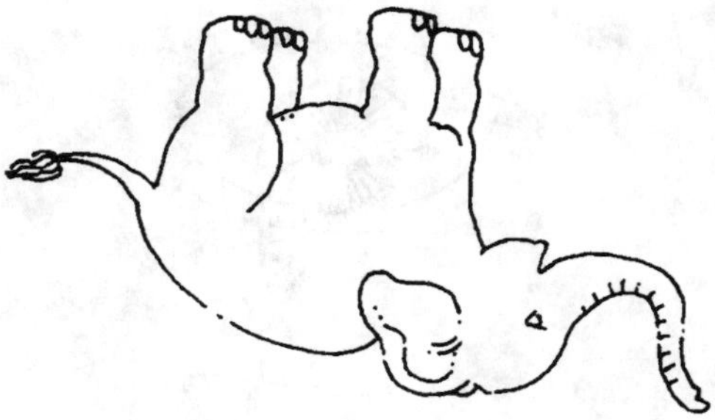

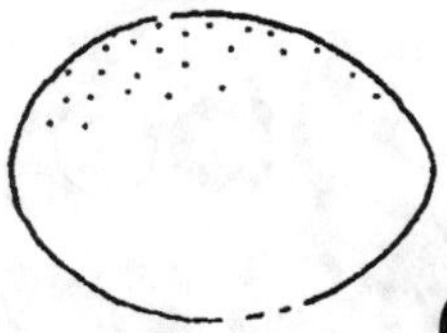

egg

E

e

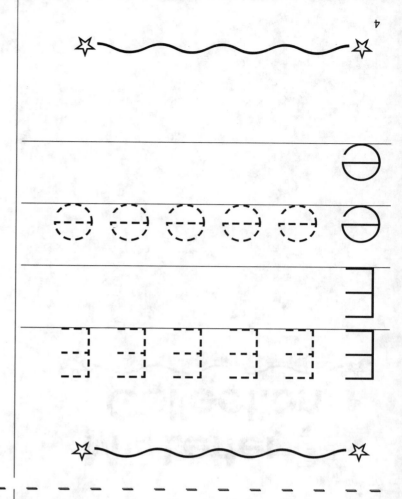

My Letter Ee
Word Bank

______'s
Letter
Ee
Book

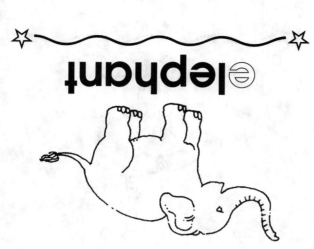

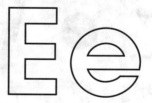

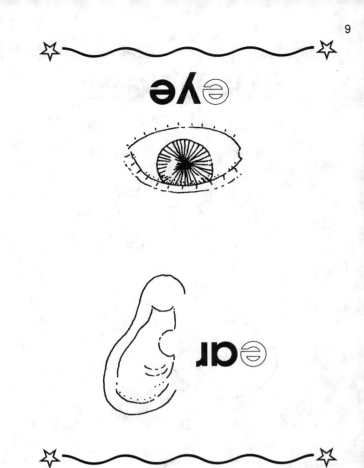

My Letter Ee Collection

Letter Ee Collection

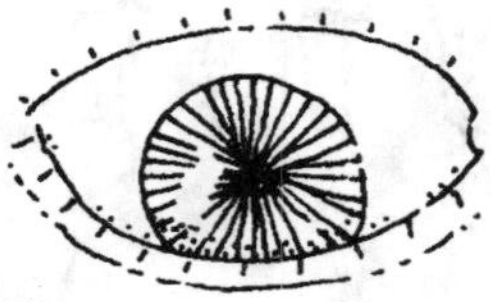

eye

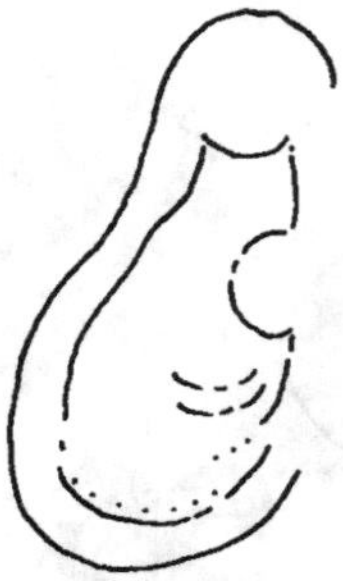

ear

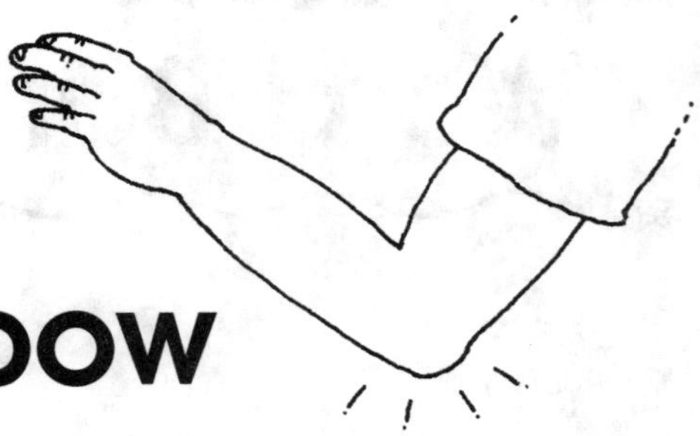

elbow

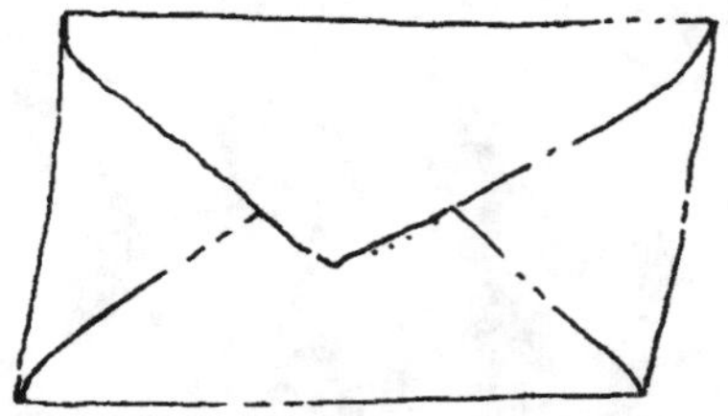

envelope

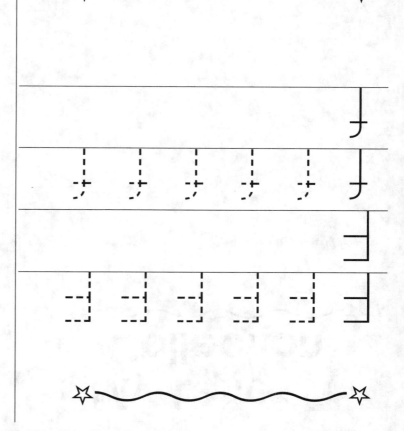

My Letter Ff Word Bank

____________'s

Letter Ff Book

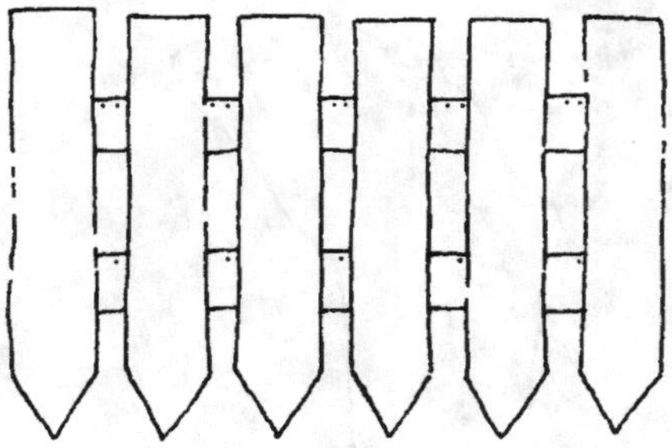

fence

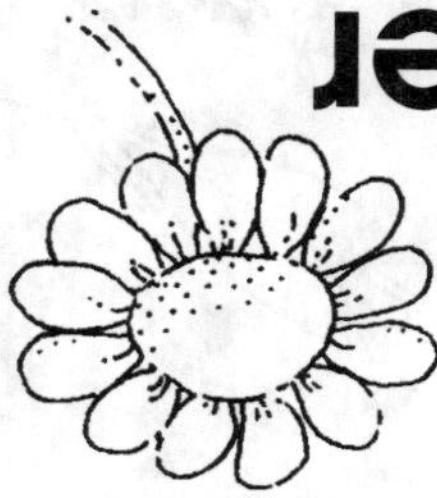

flower

Letter Ff Collection

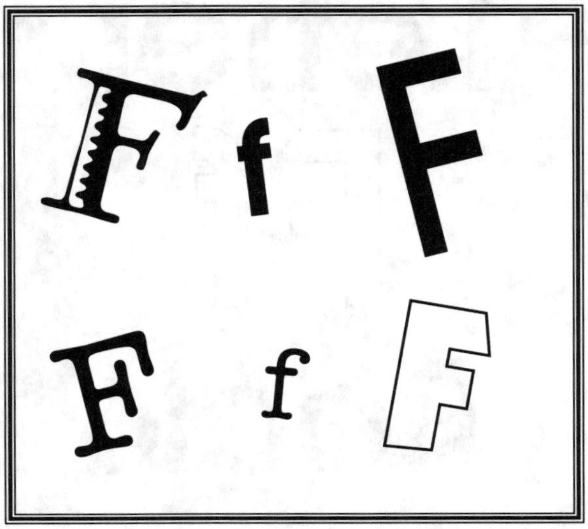

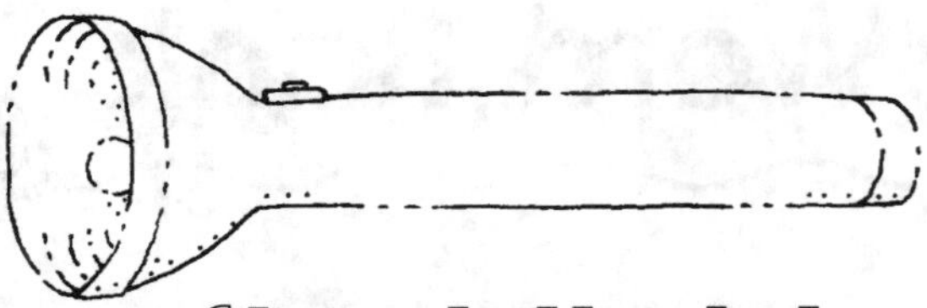

flashlight

frog

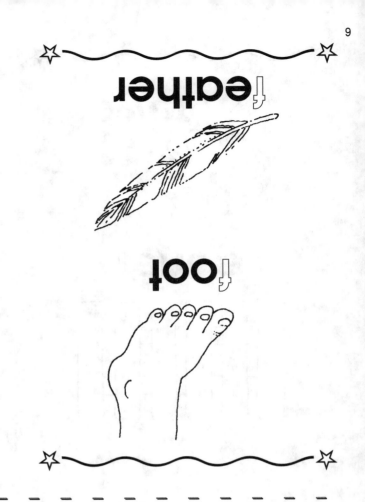

My Letter Ff Collection

feather

foot

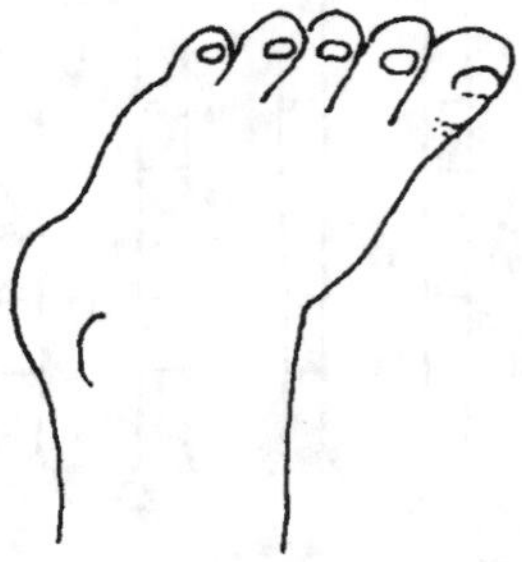

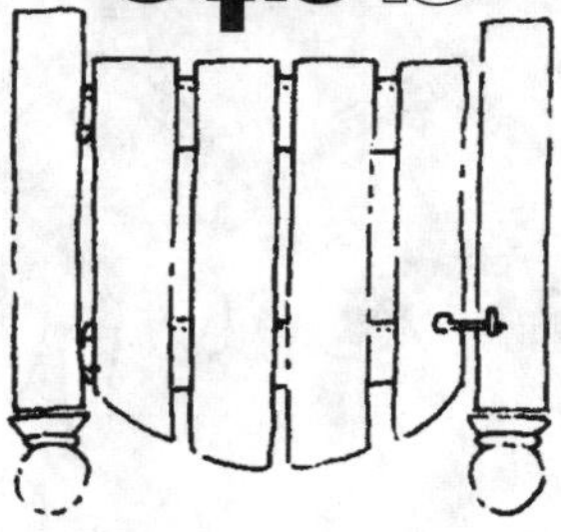

gate

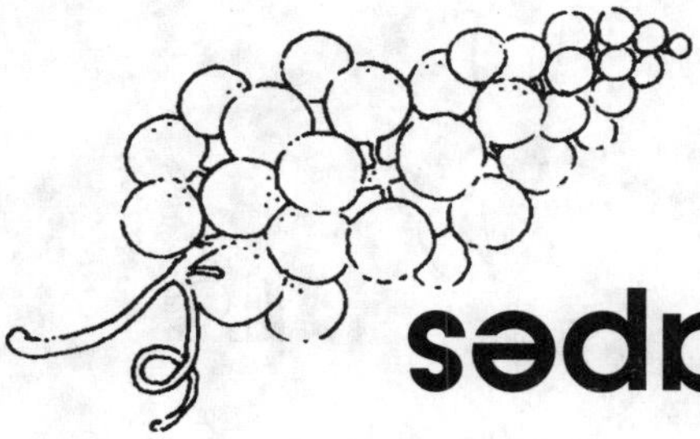

grapes

G G g g

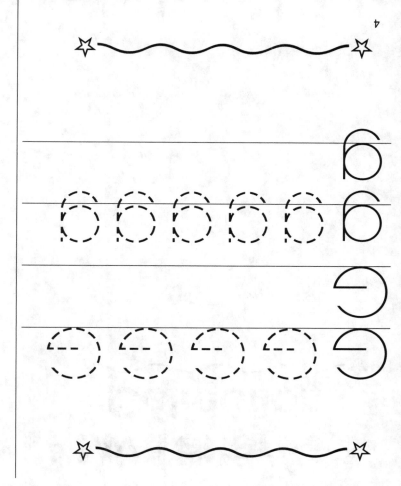

My Letter Gg Word Bank

________'s Letter Gg Book

Letter Gg Collection

G g G

G g G

My Letter Gg Collection

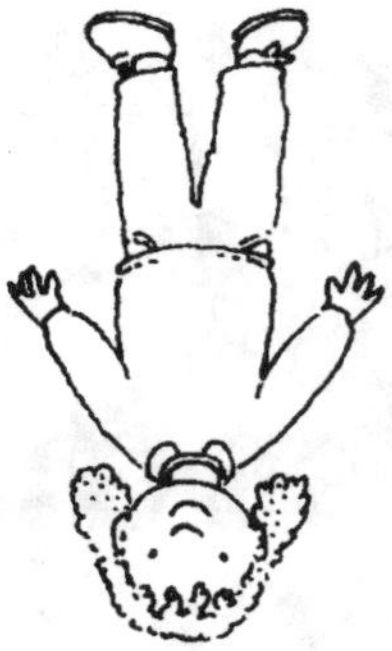

girl

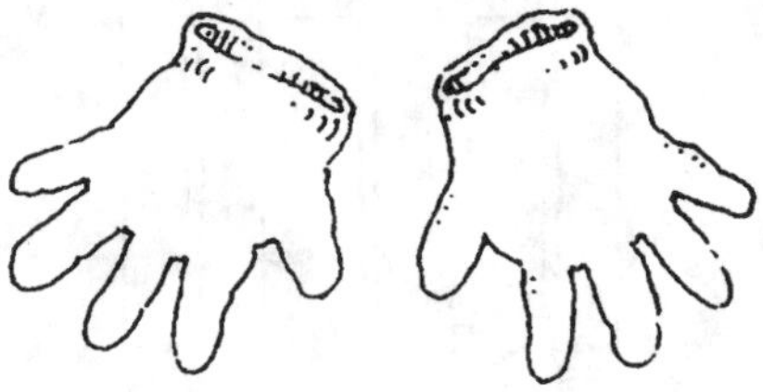

gloves

gum

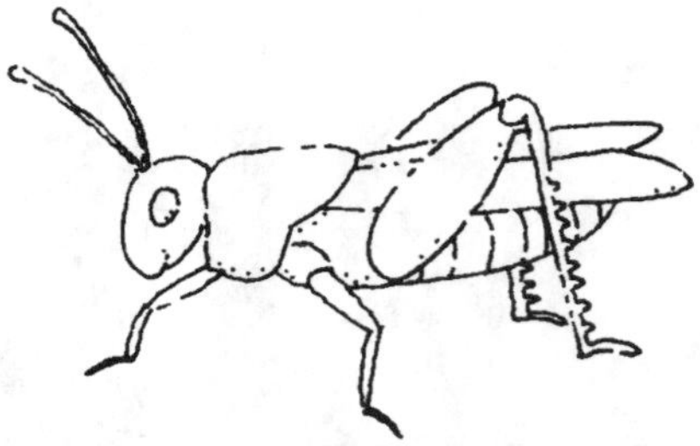

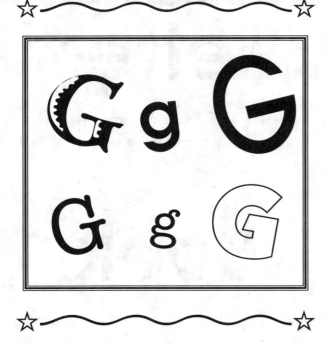

grasshopper

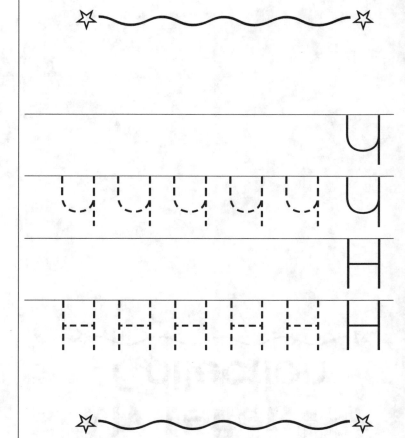

My Letter Hh
Word Bank

______'s
Letter Hh Book

H H H H H H
H
h h h h h h
h

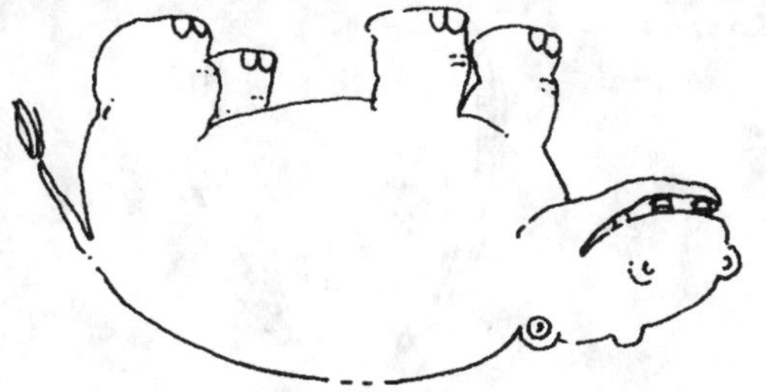
hippopotamus

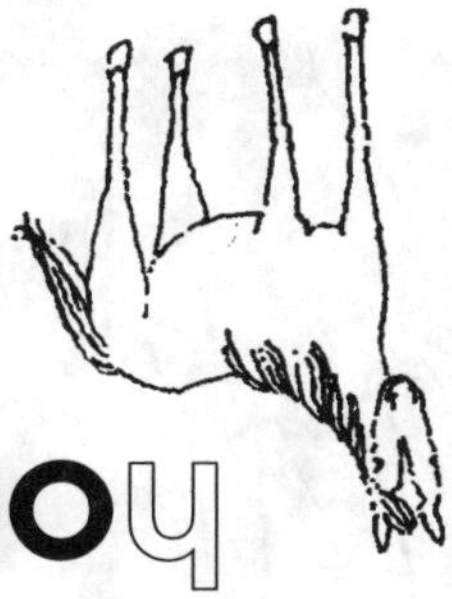
horse

Letter Hh Collection

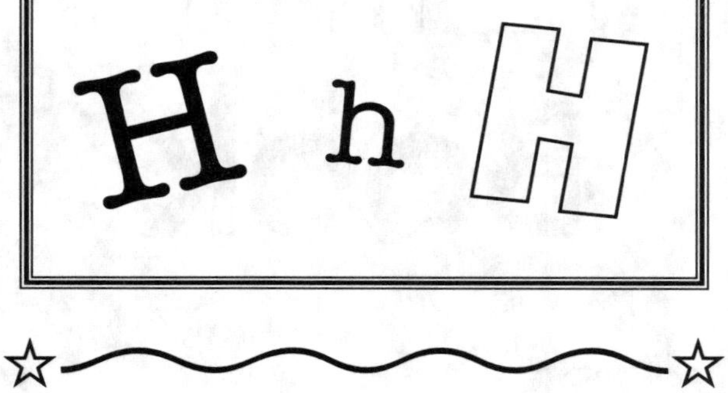

My Letter Hh Collection

hair

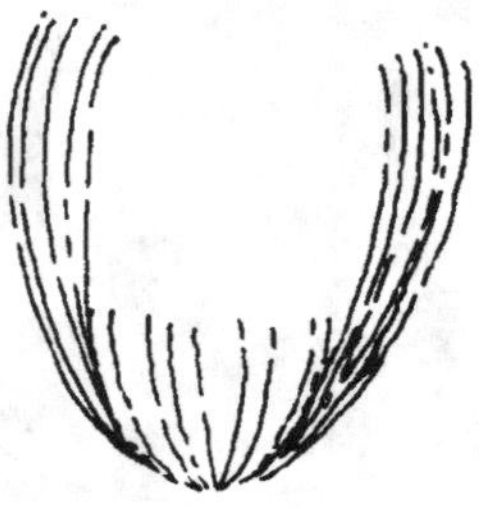

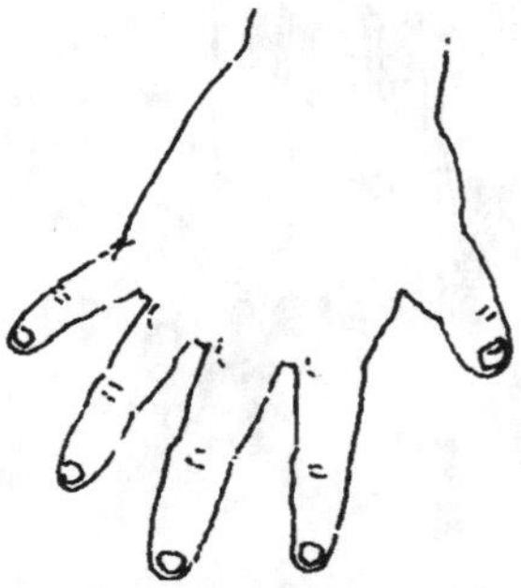

hand

hanger

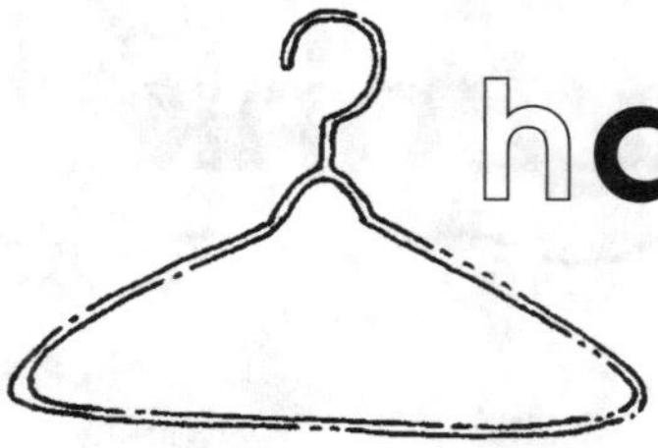

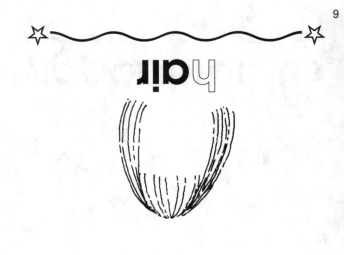

house

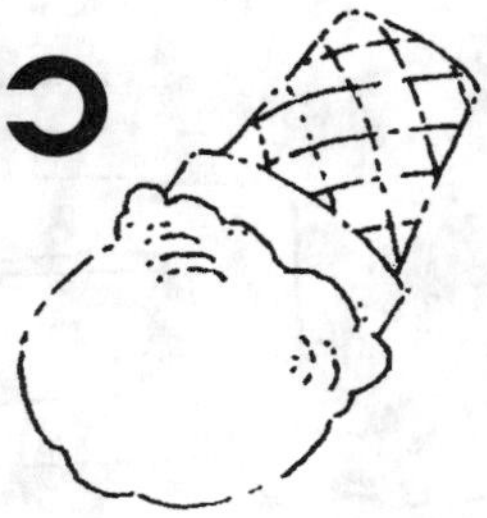

ice cream

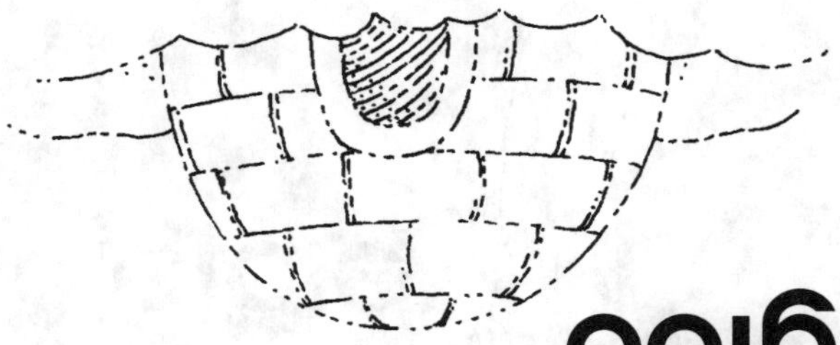

igloo

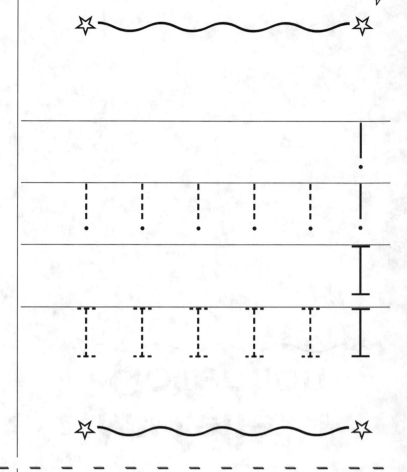

My Letter Ii Word Bank

____________'s Letter Ii Book

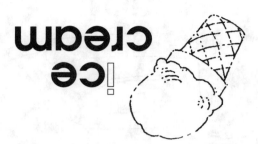

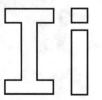

Letter Ii
Collection

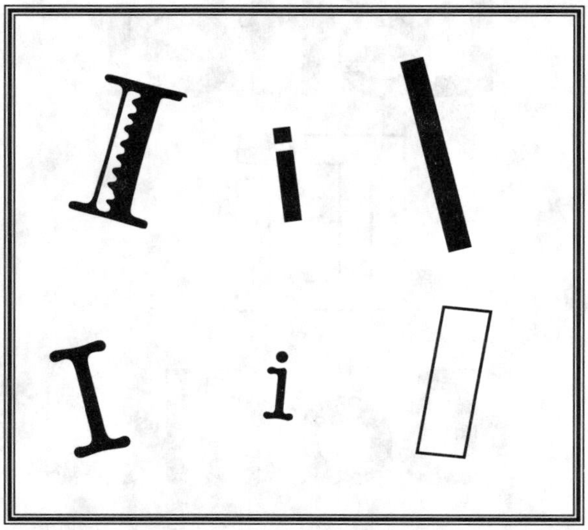

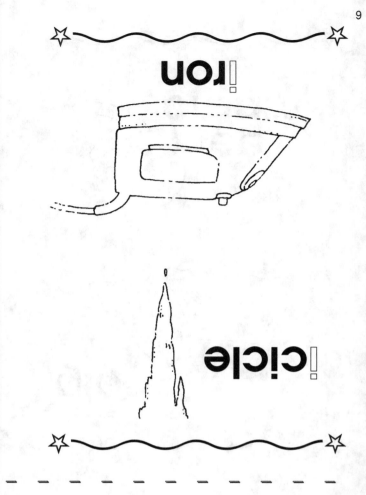

My Letter Ii
Collection

icicle

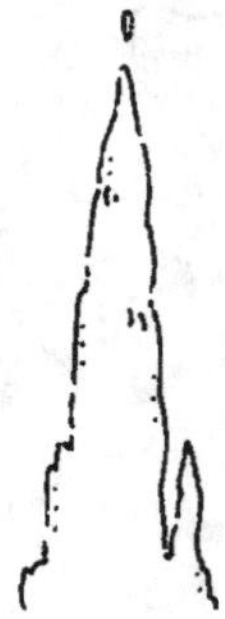

iron

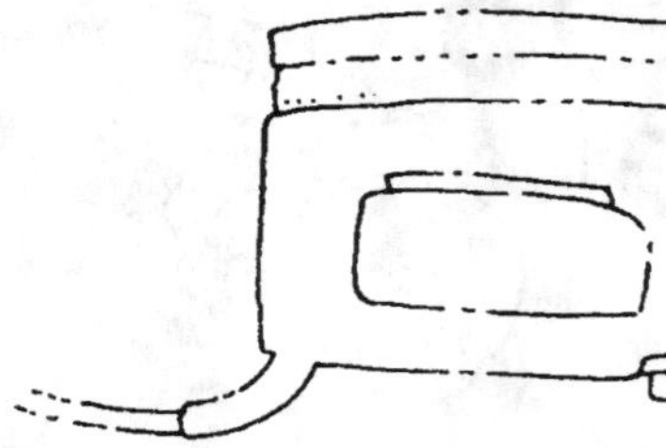

insects

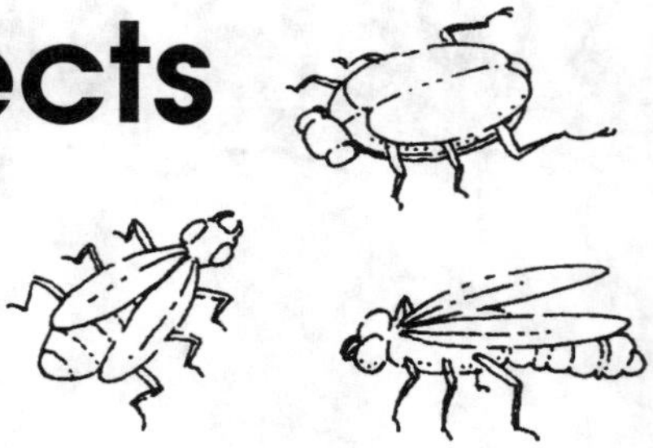

inchworm

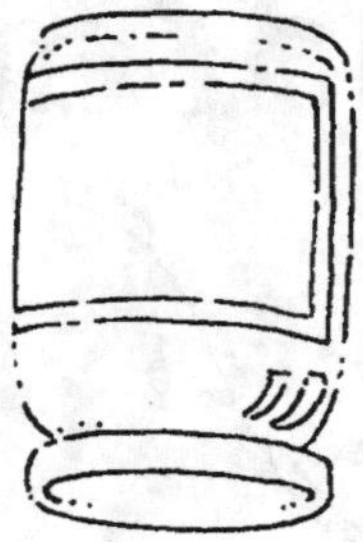

jar

jack-o'-lantern

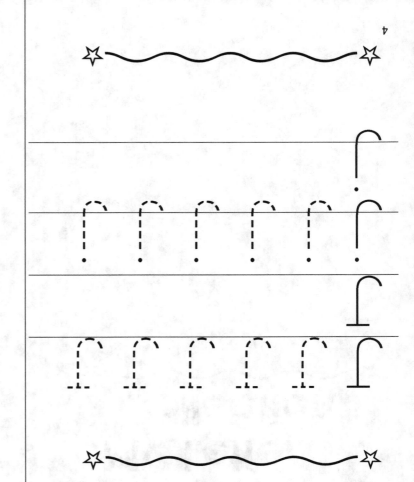

J

j

My Letter Jj Word Bank

______'s

Letter Jj Book

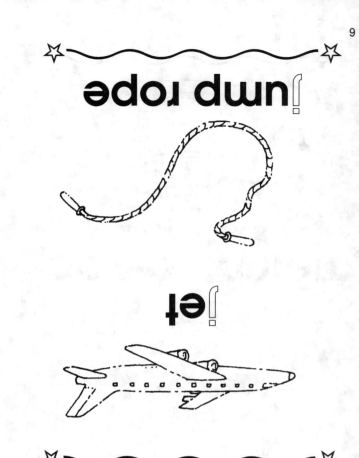

My Letter Jj Collection

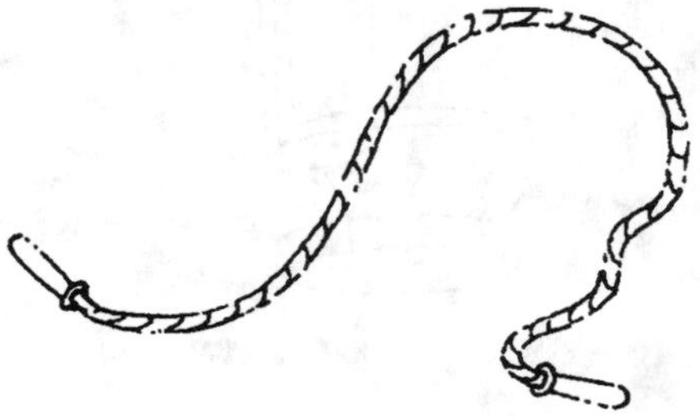

jump rope

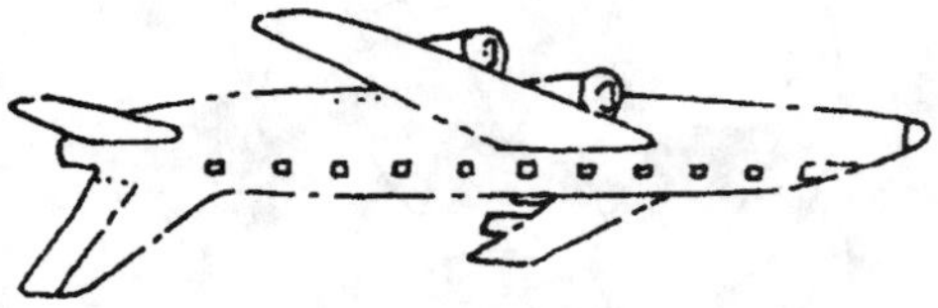

jet

Letter Jj Collection

J j J

J j J

juice box

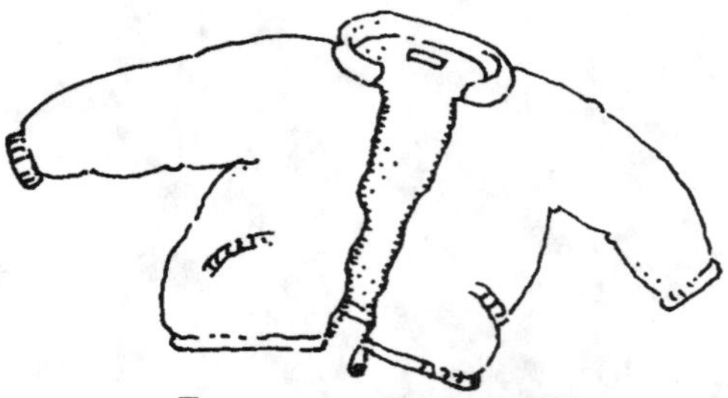

jacket

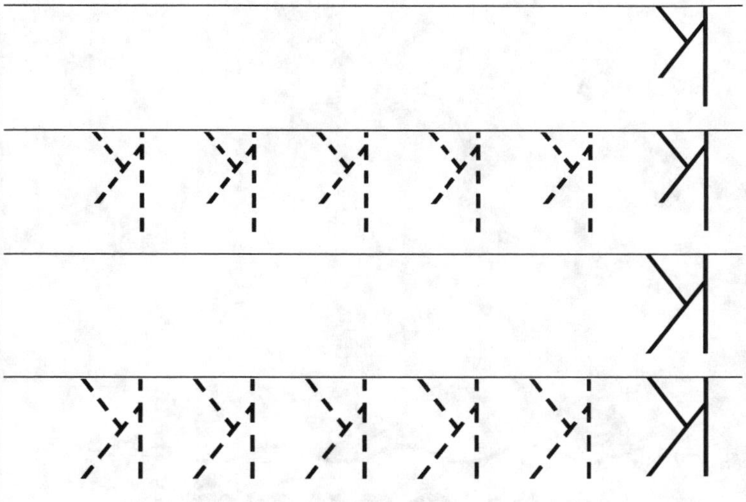

Key

Kite

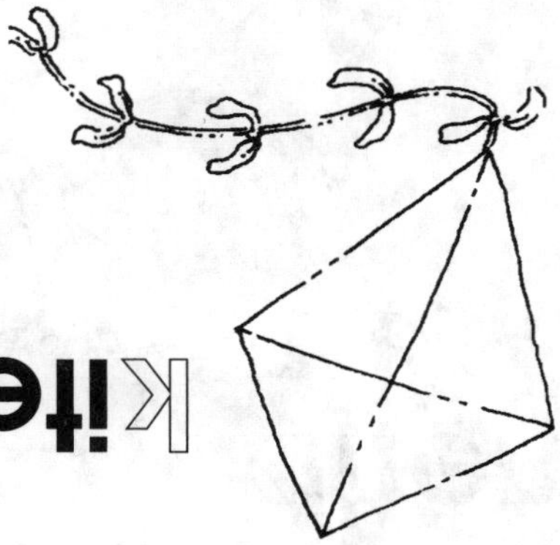

My Letter Kk Word Bank

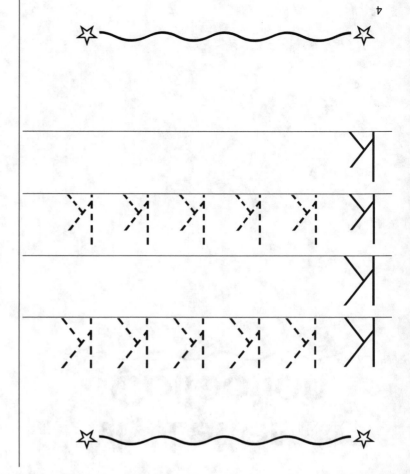

________'s Letter Kk Book

My Letter Kk Collection

king

kitten

Letter Kk Collection

K k K
K k K

kangaroo

koala bear

leaf

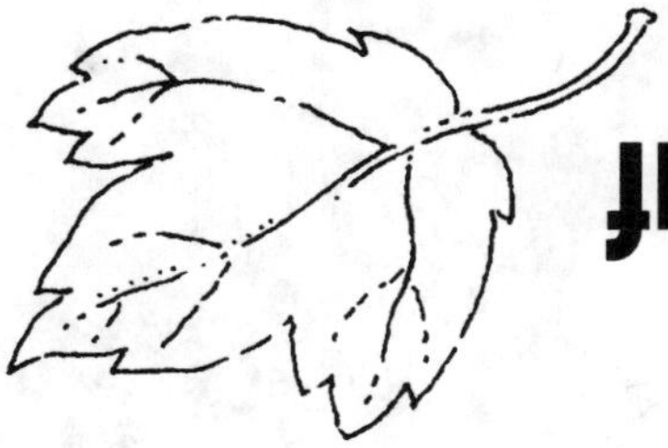

ladybug

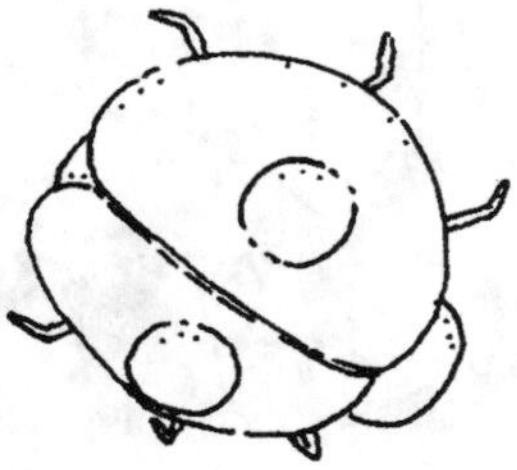

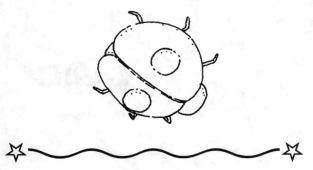

My Letter Ll Word Bank

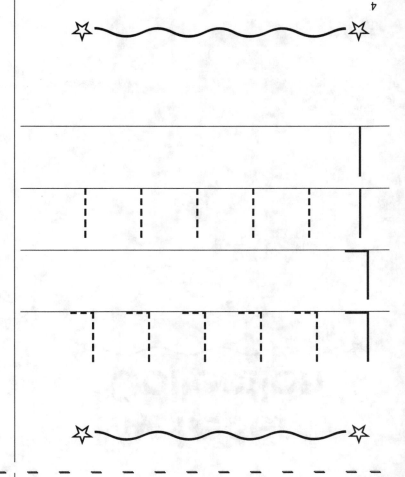

______'s Letter Ll Book

My Letter Ll Collection

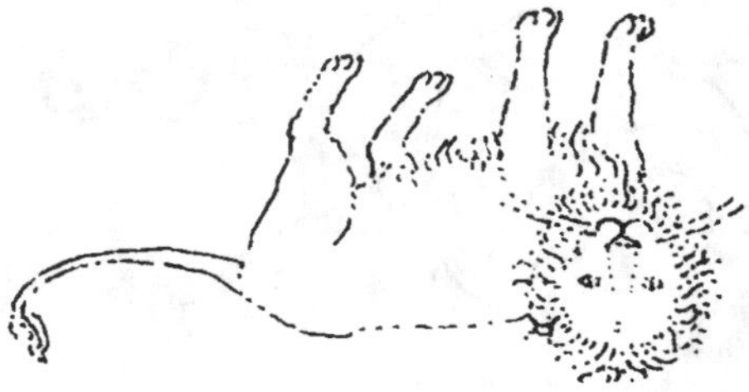

lion

lamb

Letter Ll Collection

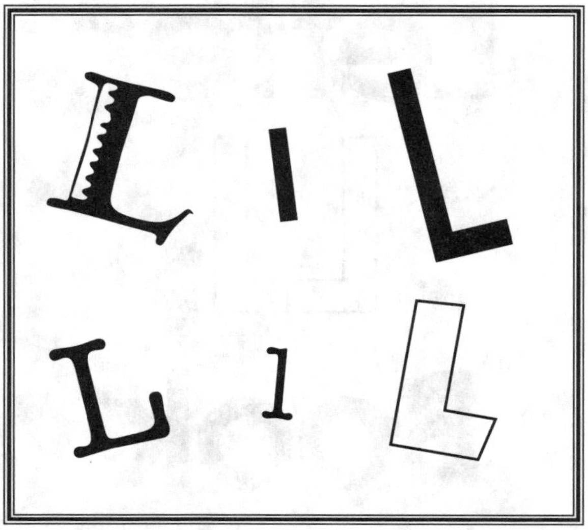

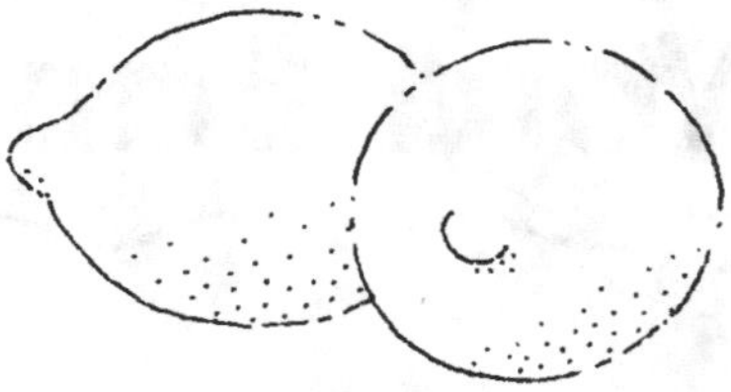

lemons

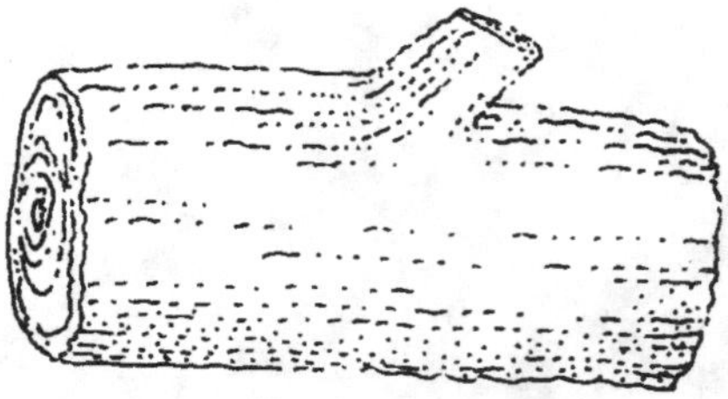

log

mouse

mitten

M M M M M M
M
m m m m m m
m

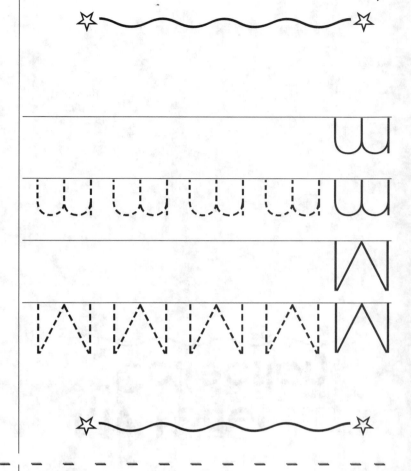

My Letter Mm Word Bank

______________'s

Letter Mm Book

My Letter Mm Collection

mop

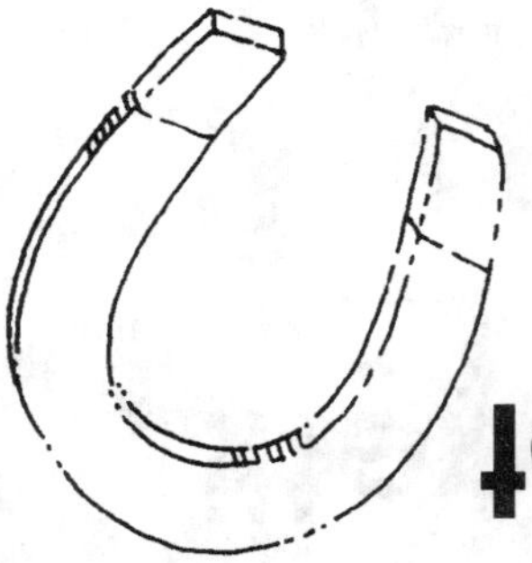

magnet

Letter Mm Collection

mailbox

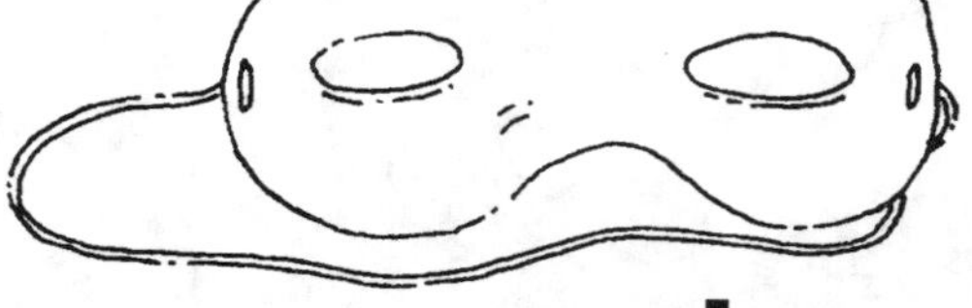

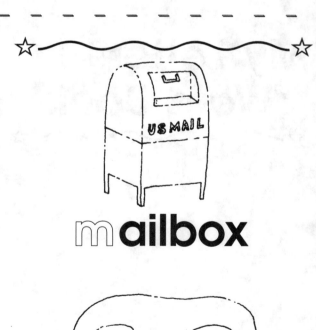

mask

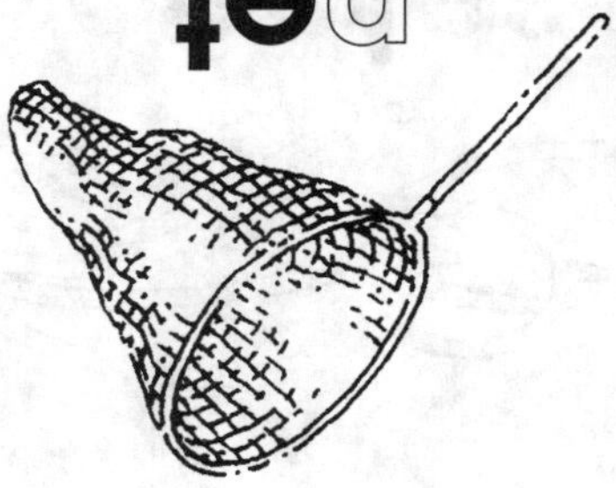

net

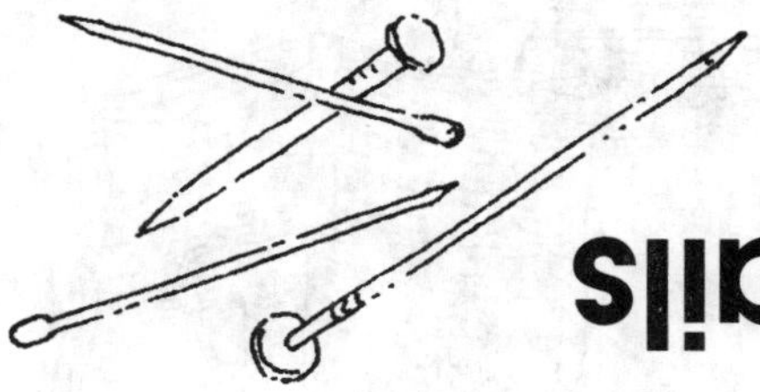

nails

N N N N N N

N

n n n n n n

n

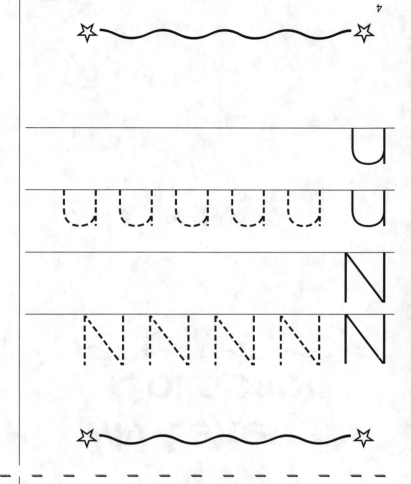

My Letter Nn Word Bank

______'s Letter Nn Book

My Letter Nn Collection

noodles

newspaper

Letter Nn Collection

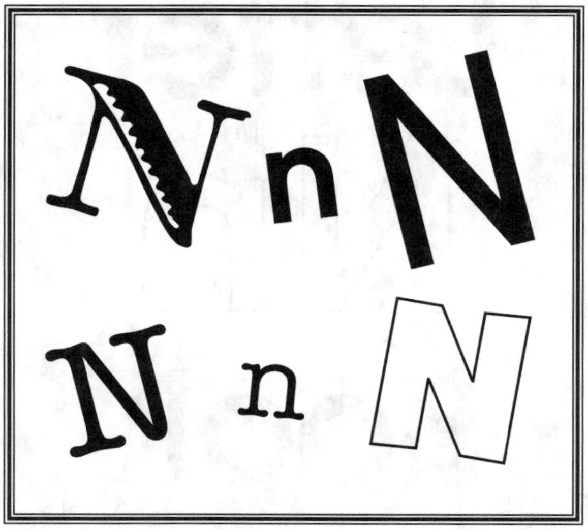

nest

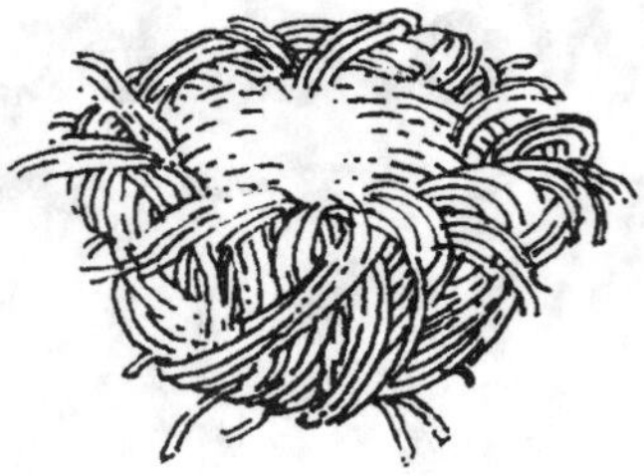

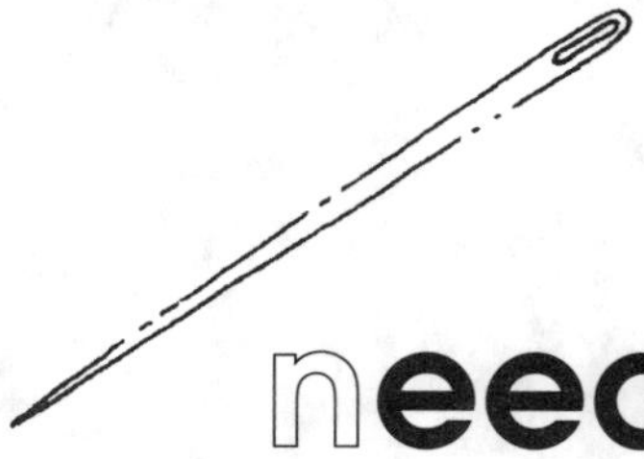

needle

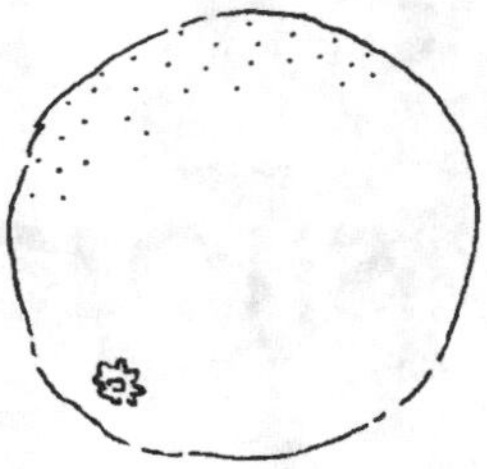

Orange

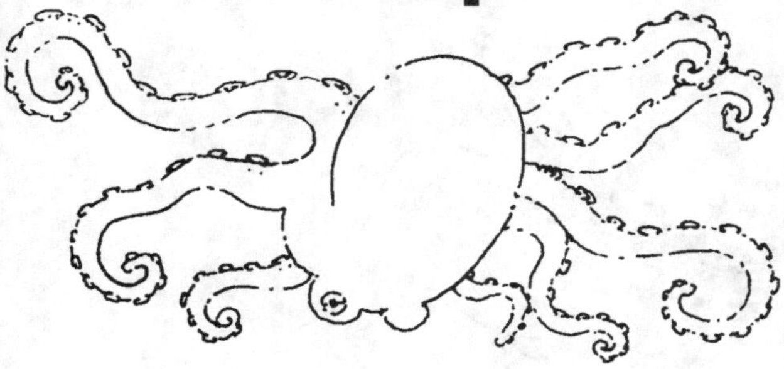

Octopus

My Letter Oo Word Bank

_______'s Letter Oo Book

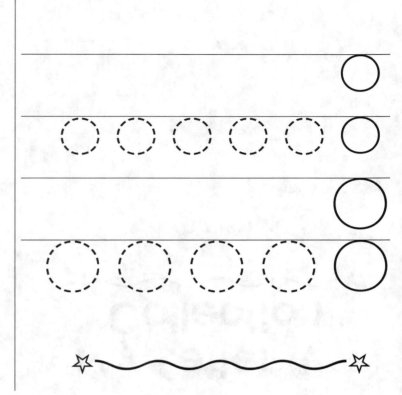

Letter Oo Collection

O o O
O o O

My Letter Oo Collection

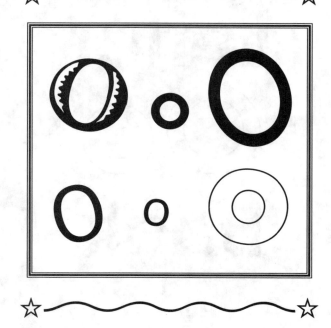

ostrich

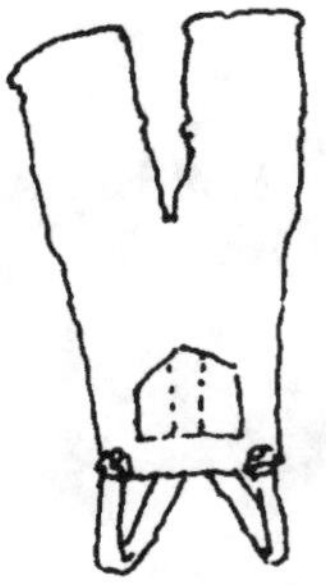

overalls

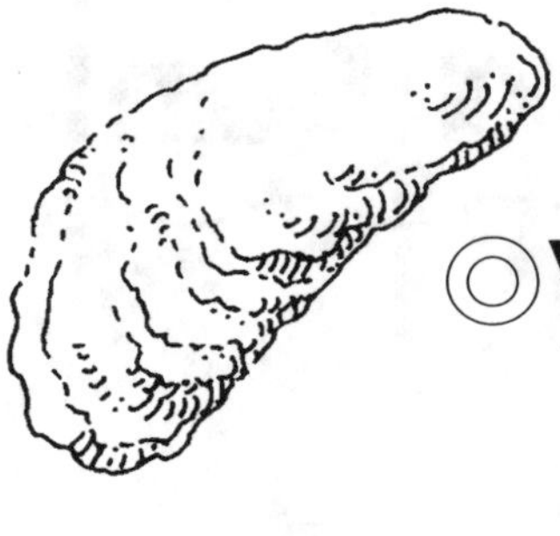

oyster

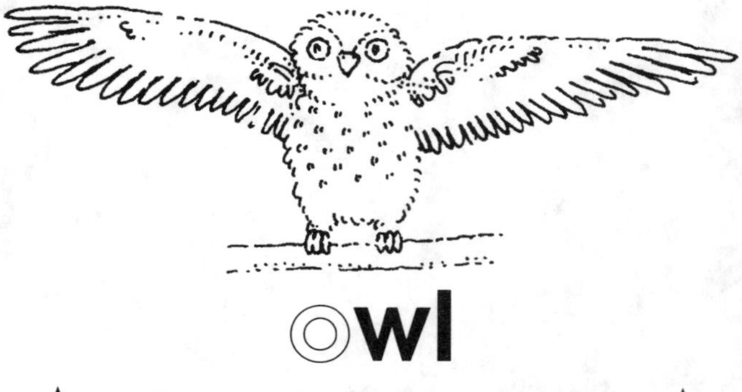

owl

____________'s

Letter Pp Book

My Letter Pp Word Bank

paint

paint brush

My Letter Pp Collection

penguin

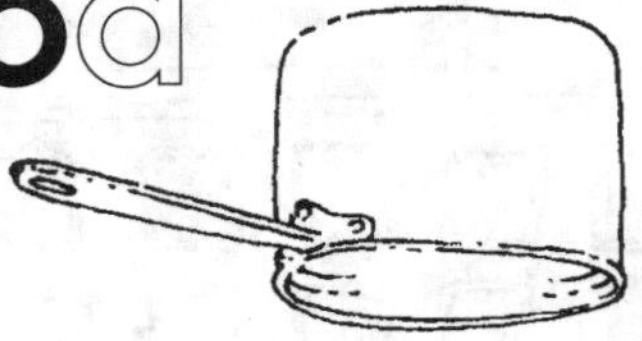

pot

Letter Pp Collection

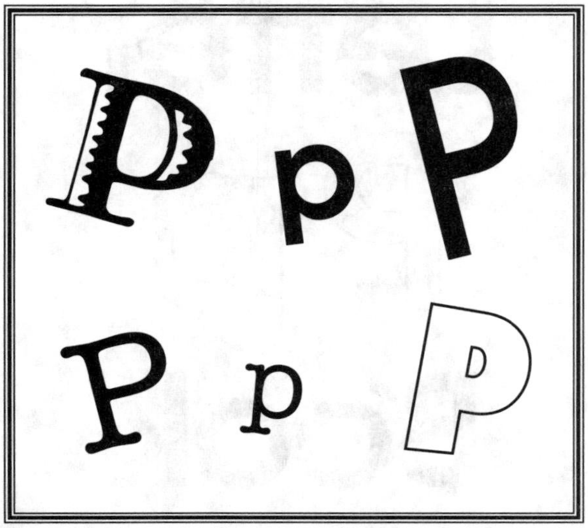

pig

pie

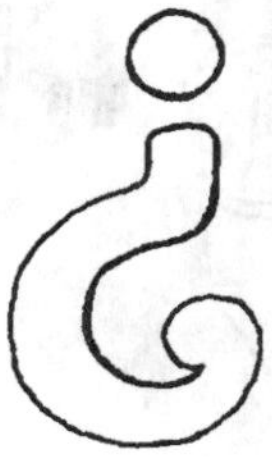

question mark

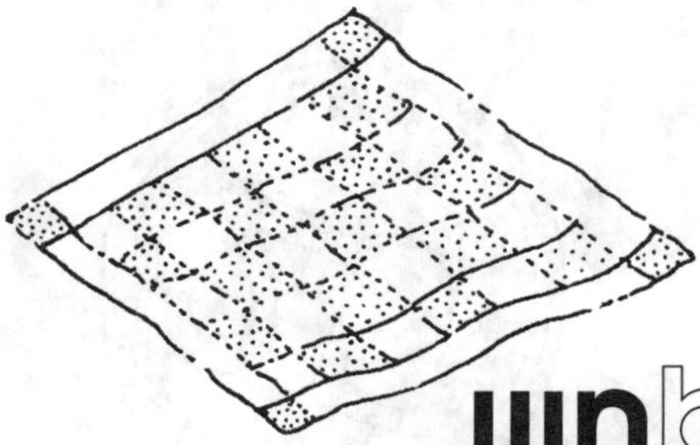

quilt

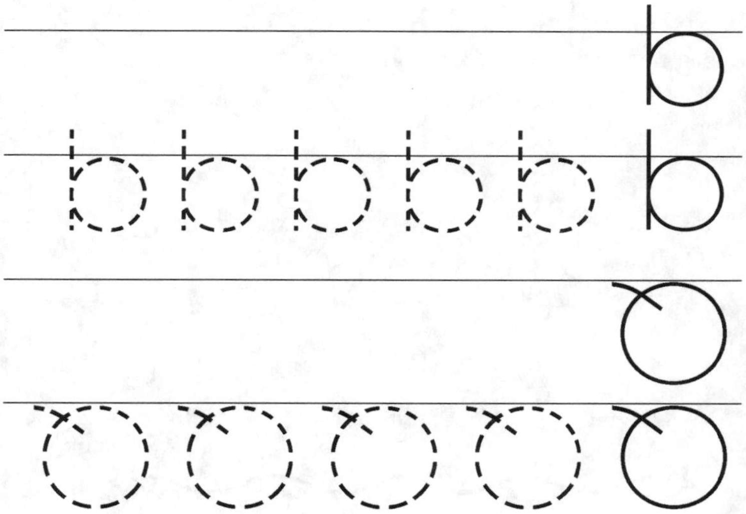

My Letter Qq Word Bank

______'s

Letter Qq Book

Letter Qq Collection

Q q Q
Q q Q

queen

quill

My Letter Qq Collection

quart

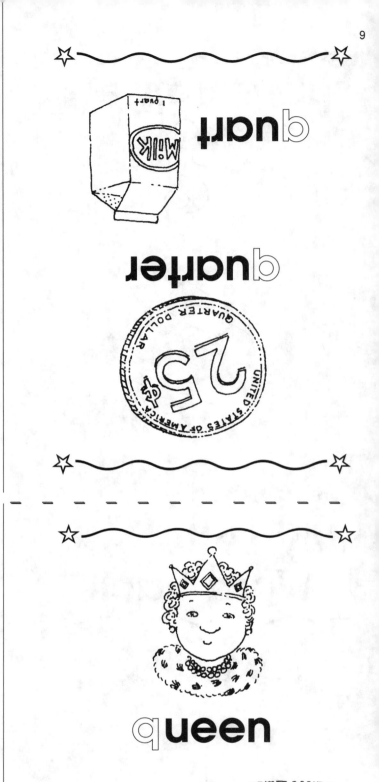

quarter

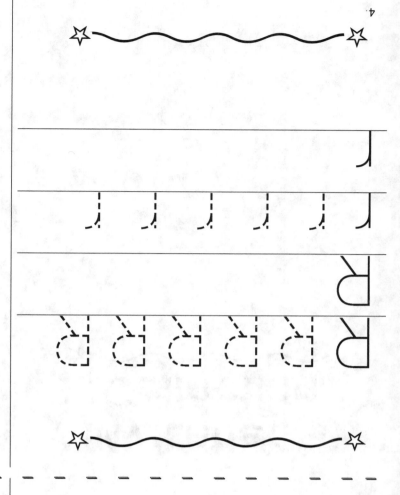

My Letter Rr
Word Bank

______'s
Letter
Rr
Book

robot

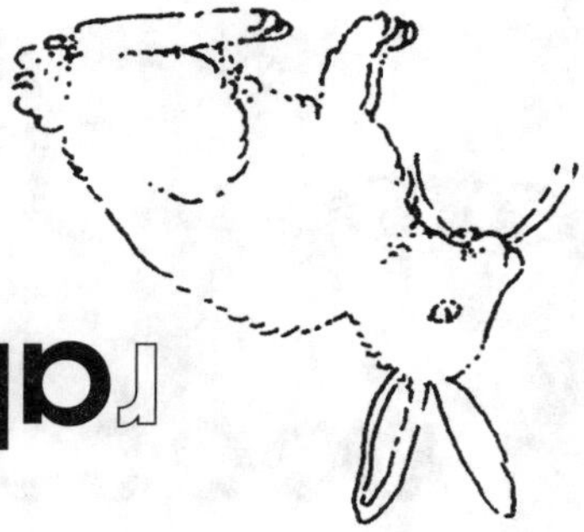

rabbit

R R R R R R

R

r r r r r r

r

My Letter Rr Collection

rainbow

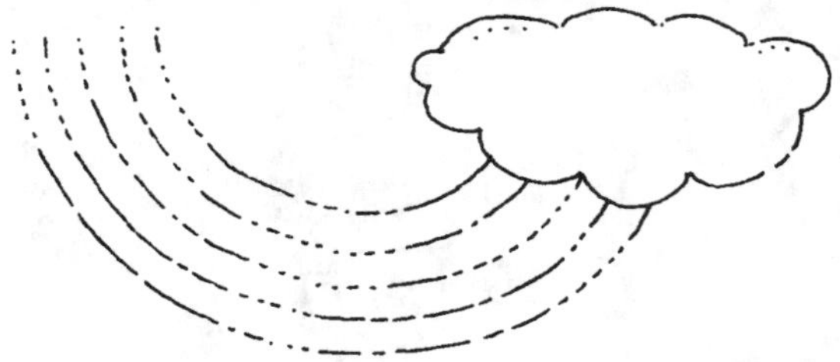

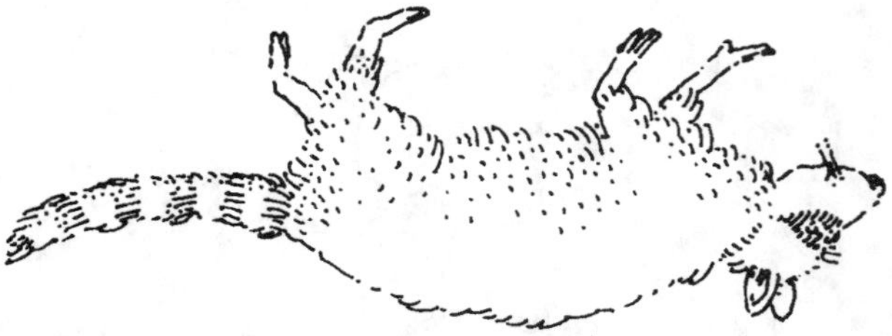

raccoon

Letter Rr Collection

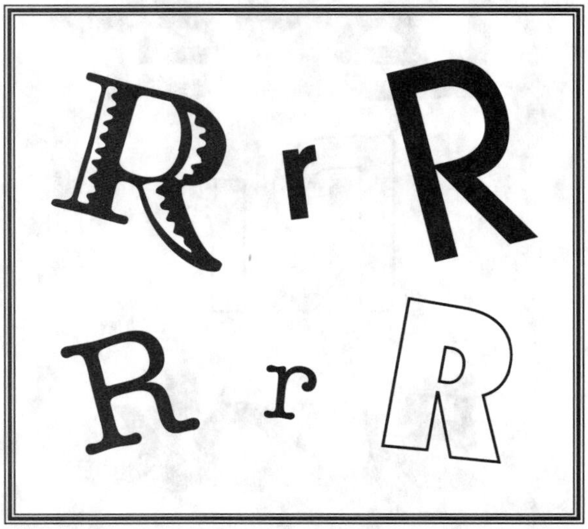

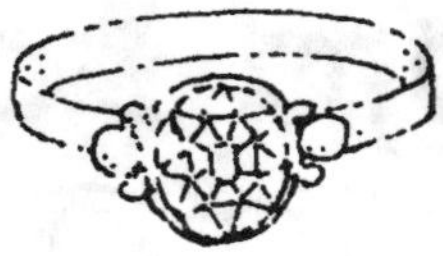

ring

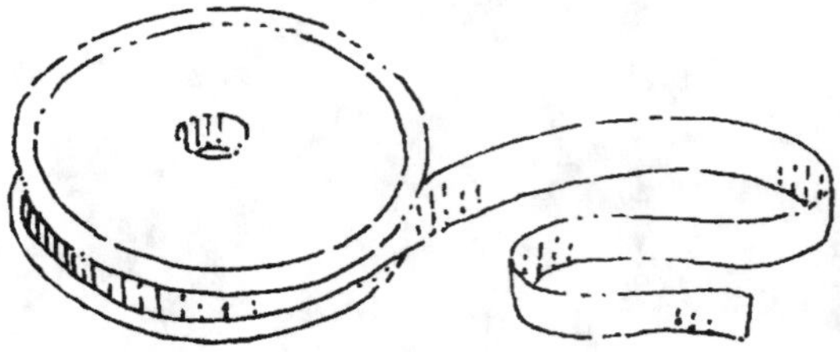

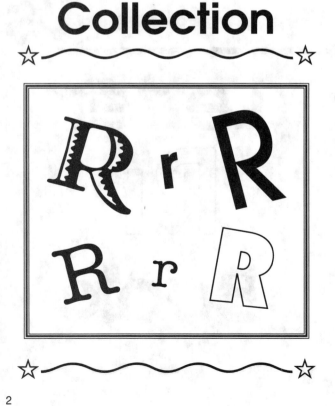

ribbon

sweater

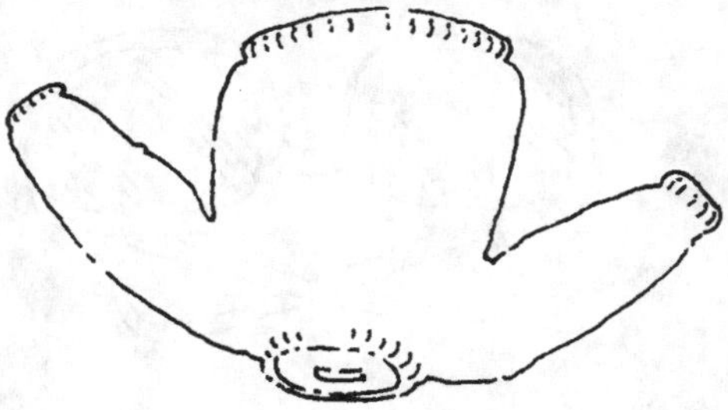

sock

s s s s s s

s

S S S S S S

S

My Letter Ss Word Bank

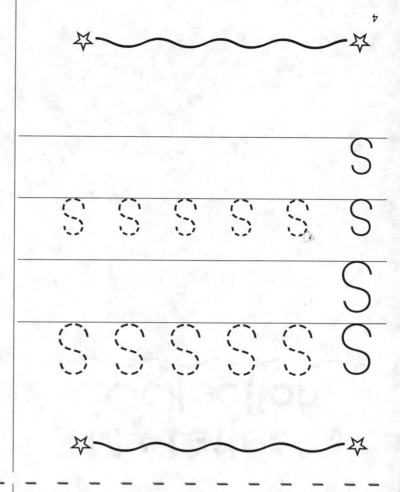

______'s Letter Ss Book

My Letter Ss Collection

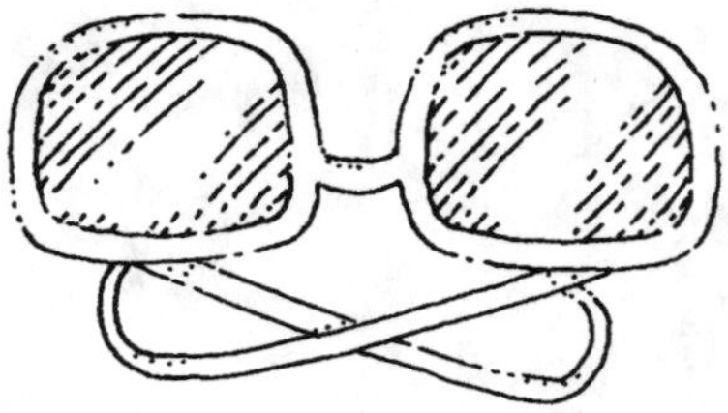

sunglasses

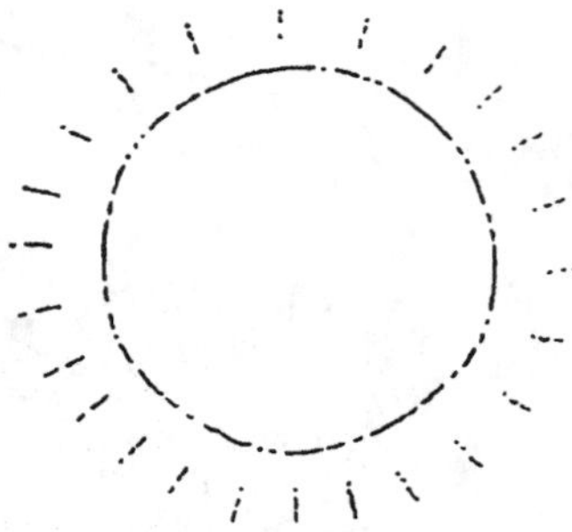

sun

Letter Ss Collection

S s S

S s S

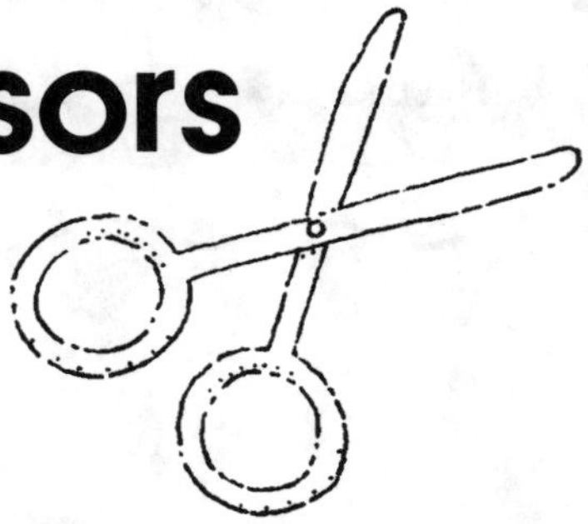

scissors

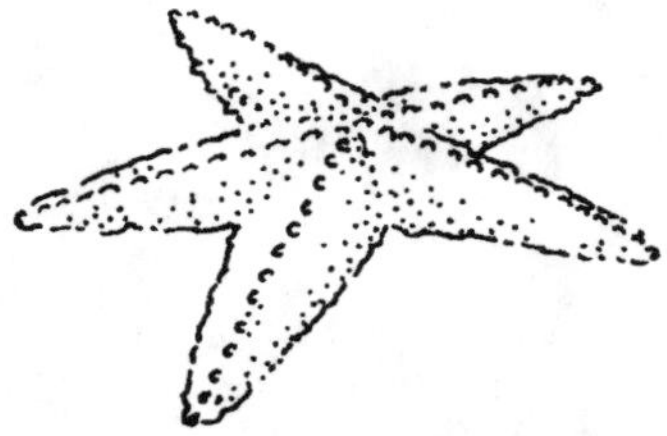

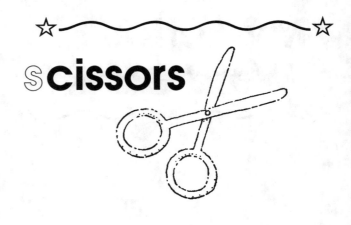

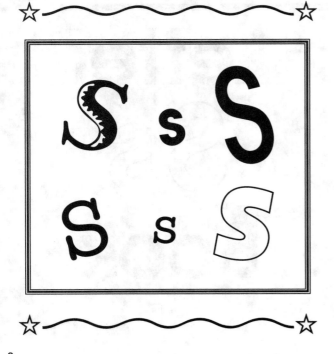

starfish

My Letter Tt Word Bank

____'s Letter Tt Book

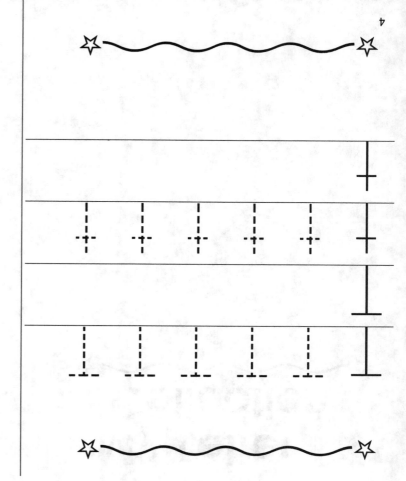

television

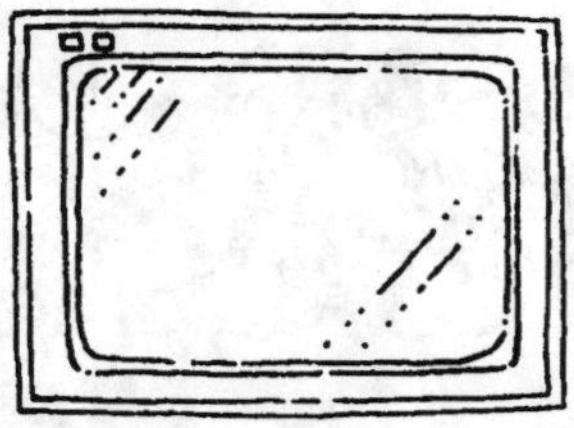

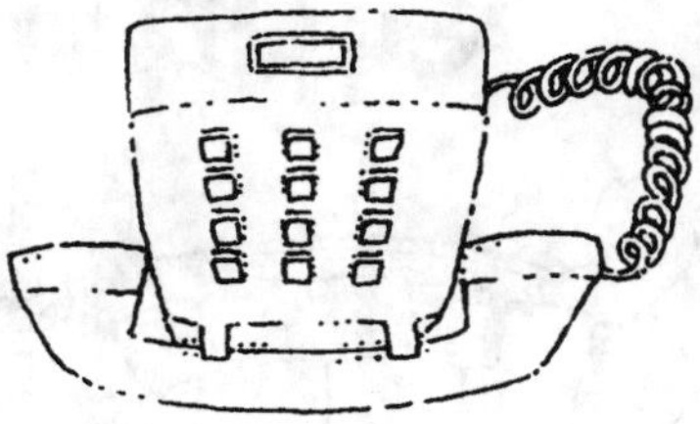

telephone

T T T T T T

t t t t t t

3

My Letter Tt Collection

Letter Tt Collection

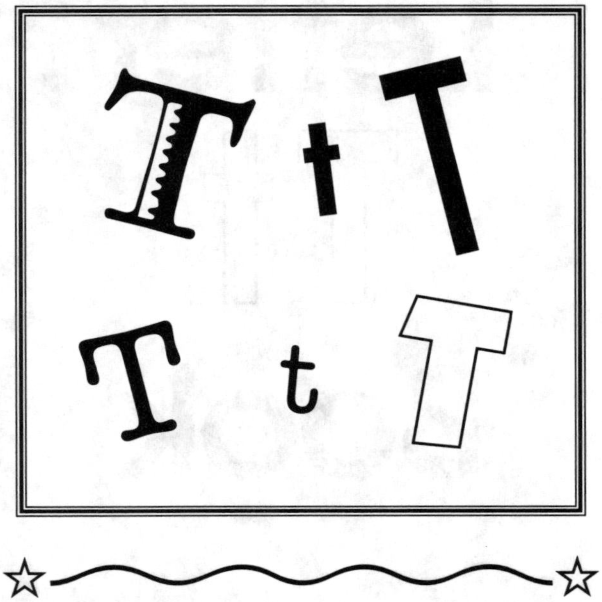

tiger

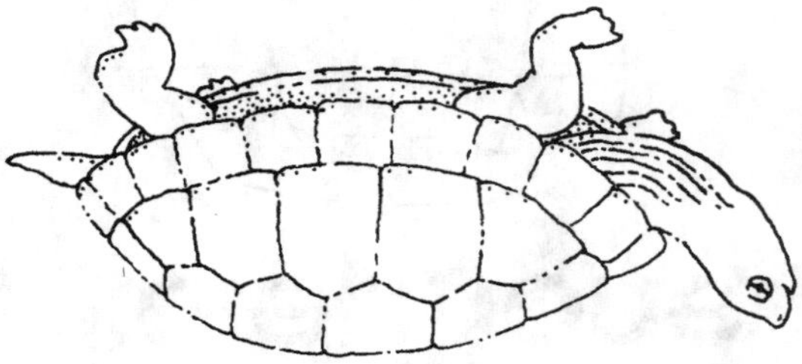

turtle

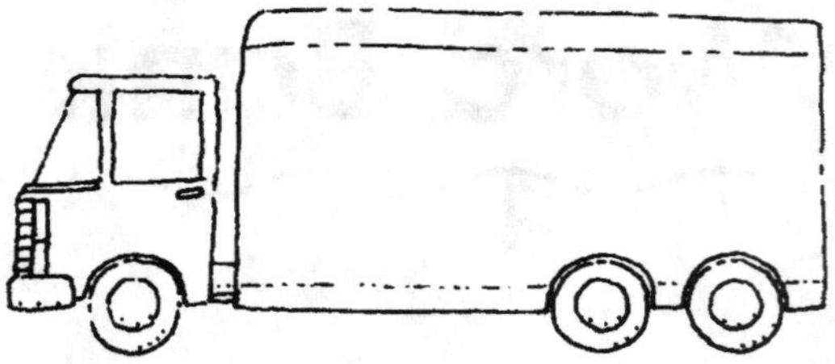

truck

teeth

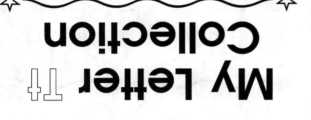

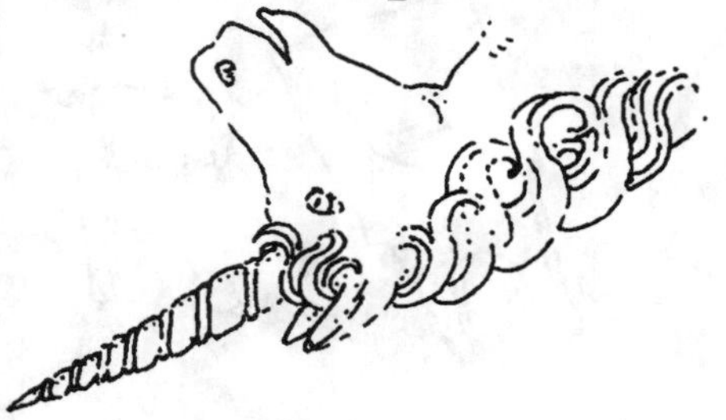

unicorn

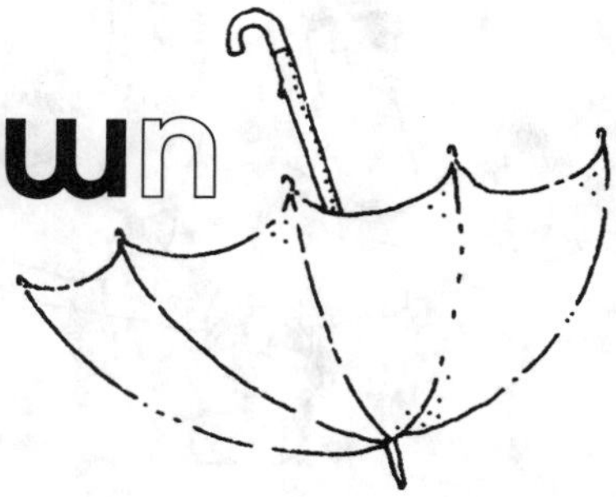

umbrella

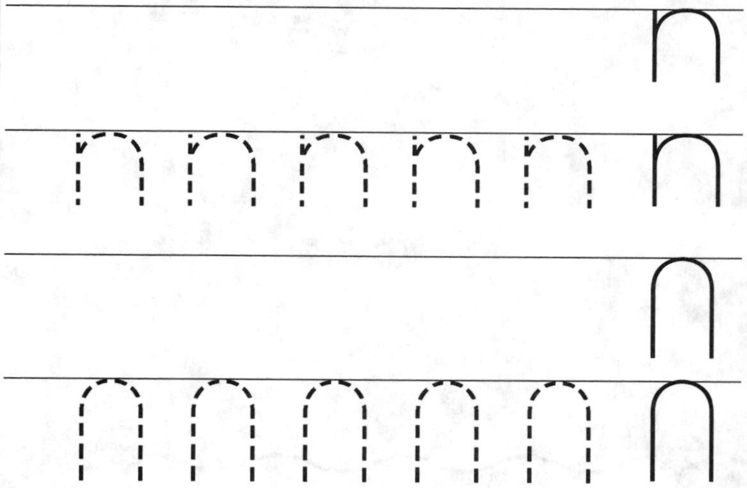

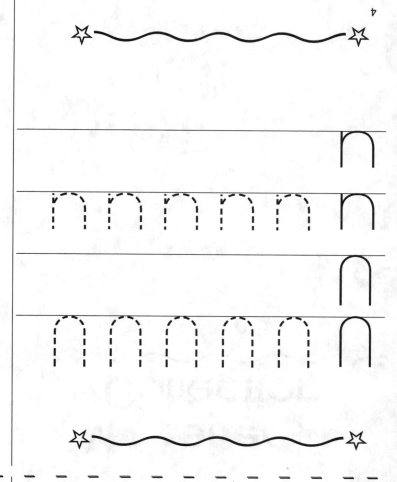

My Letter Uu Word Bank

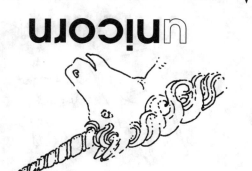

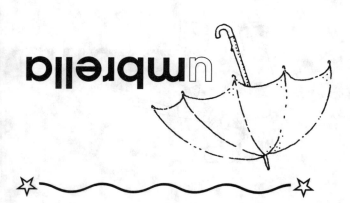

_______'s Letter Uu Book

My Letter Uu Collection

uniform

umpire

Letter Uu Collection

U u U
U u U

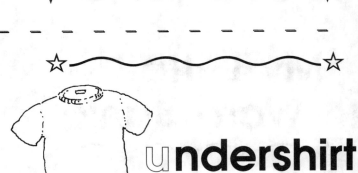

undershirt

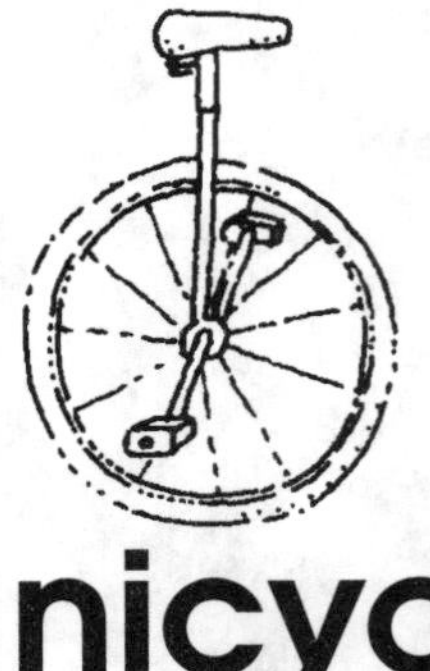

unicycle

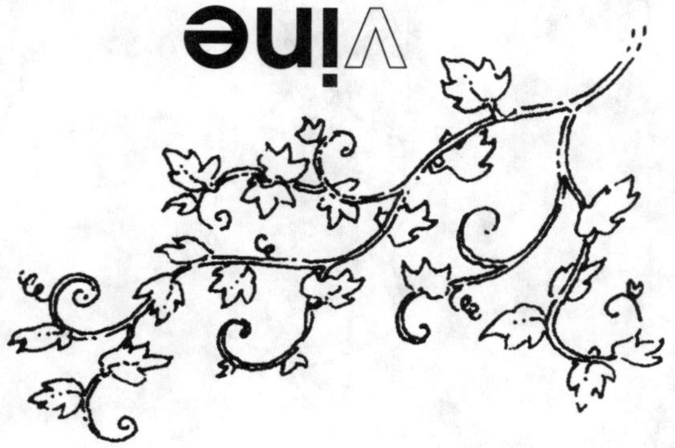

Vine

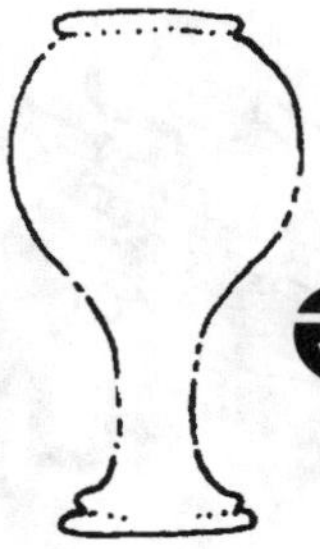

Vase

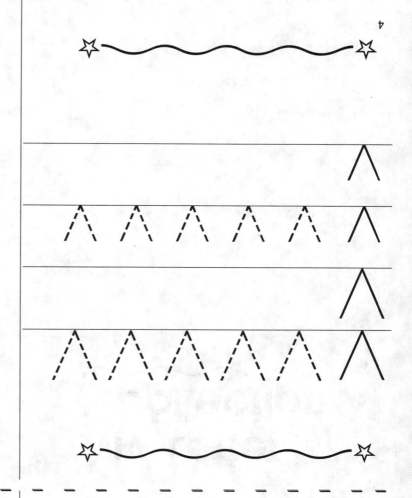

My Letter Vv Word Bank

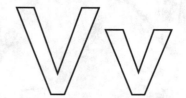

_______________'s

Letter Vv Book

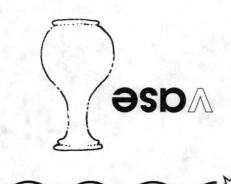

Letter Vv Collection

My Letter Vv Collection

vest

violin

valentine

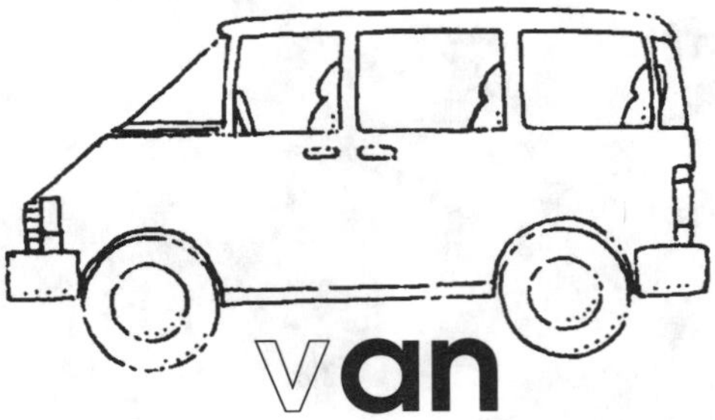

van

My Letter Ww Word Bank

_______'s

Letter Ww Book

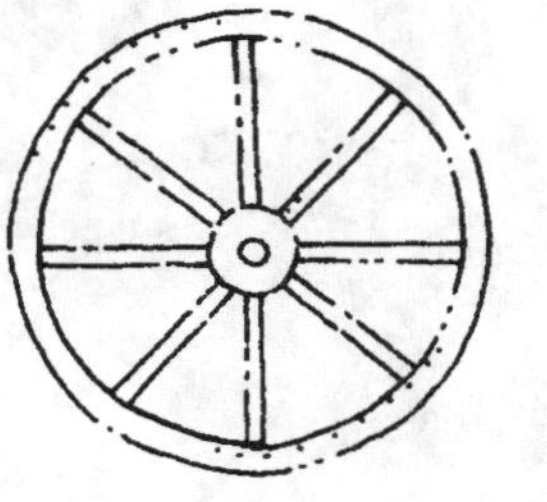

wheel

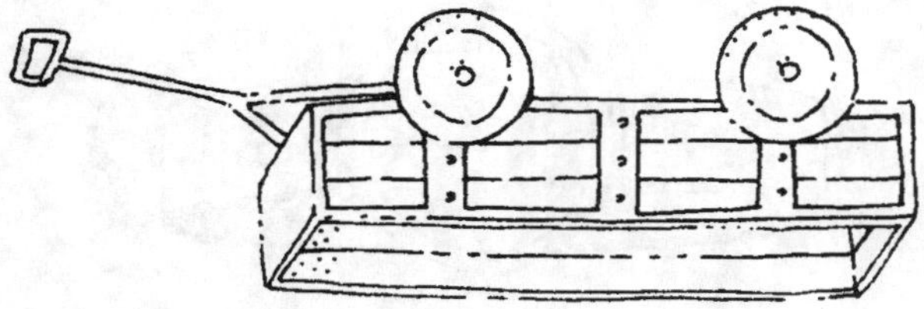

wagon

W W W W W W

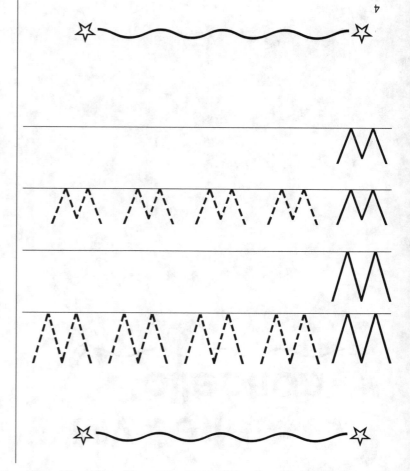

W W W W W W

Letter Ww Collection

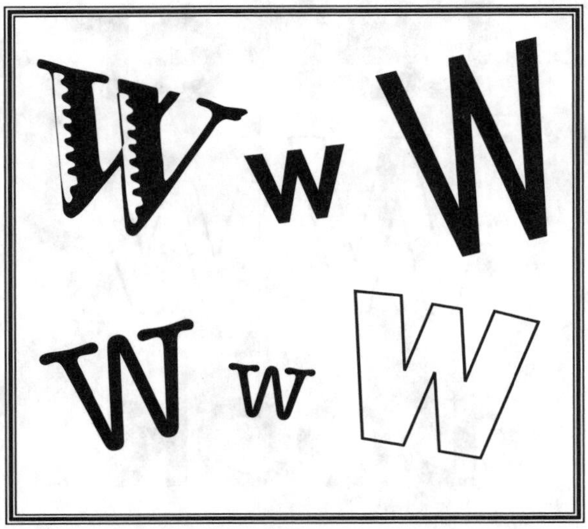

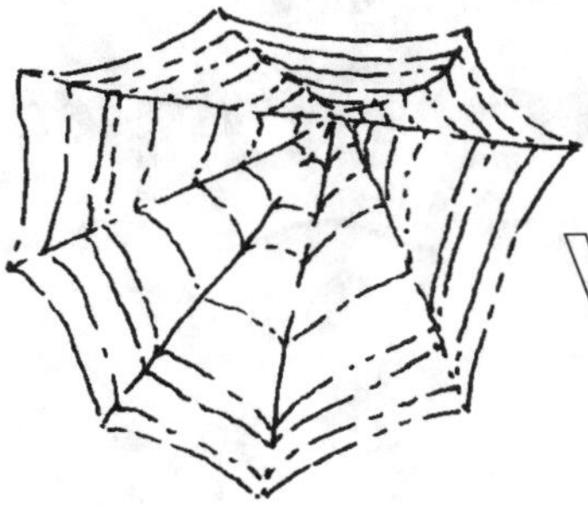

web

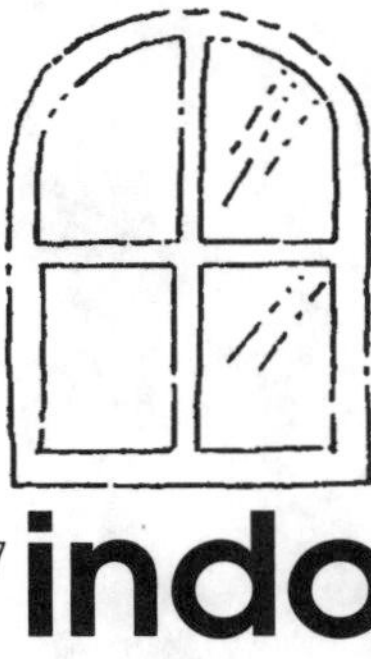

window

My Letter Ww Collection

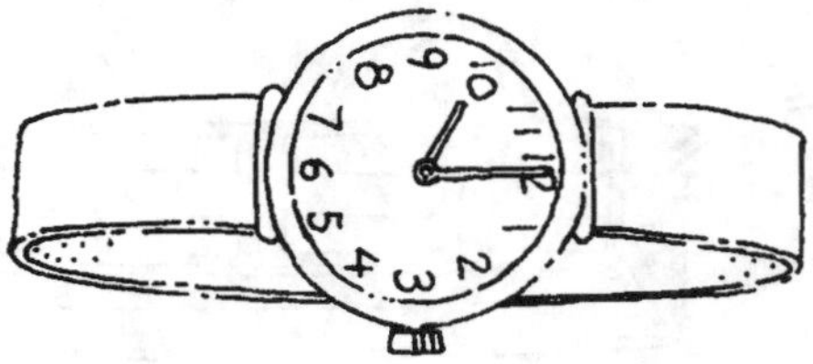

watch

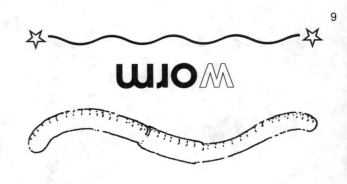

worm

X-ray

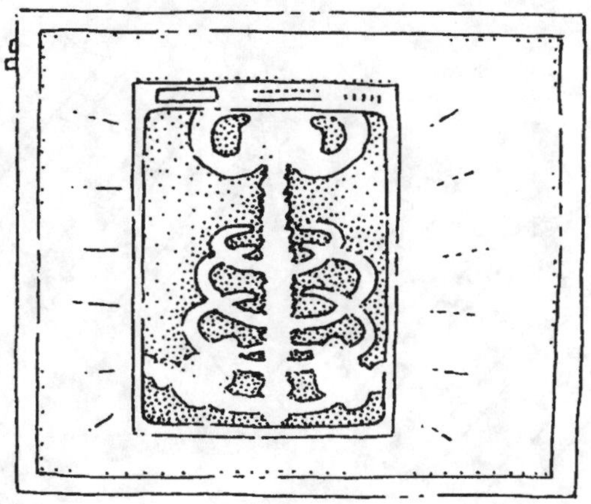

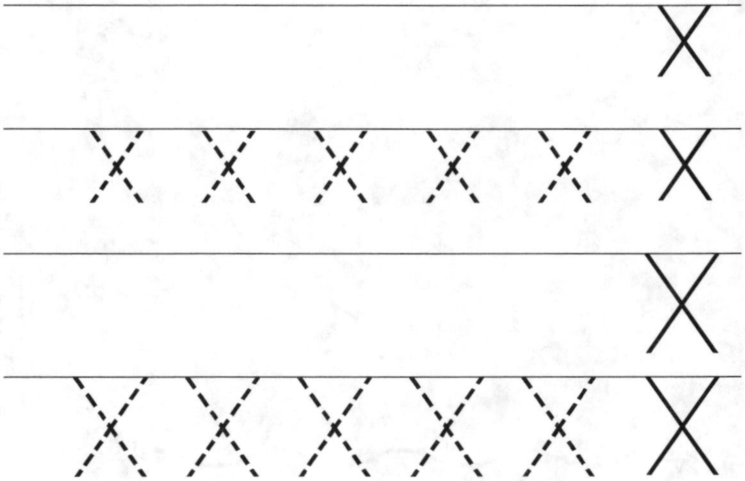

My Letter Xx Word Bank

__________'s

Letter Xx Book

My Letter Xx Collection

xylophone

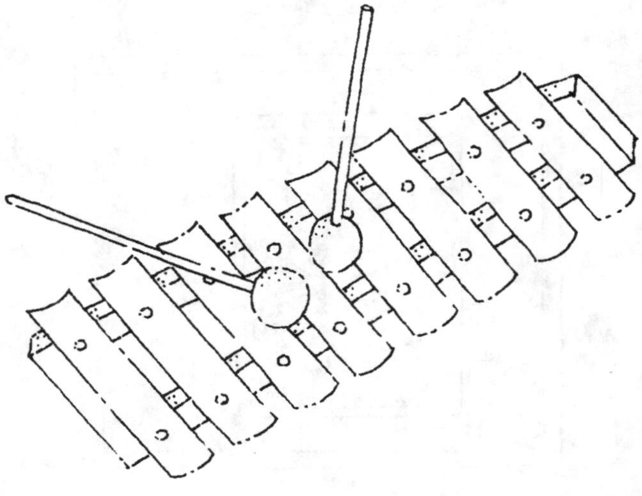

Letter Xx Collection

X x X
X x X

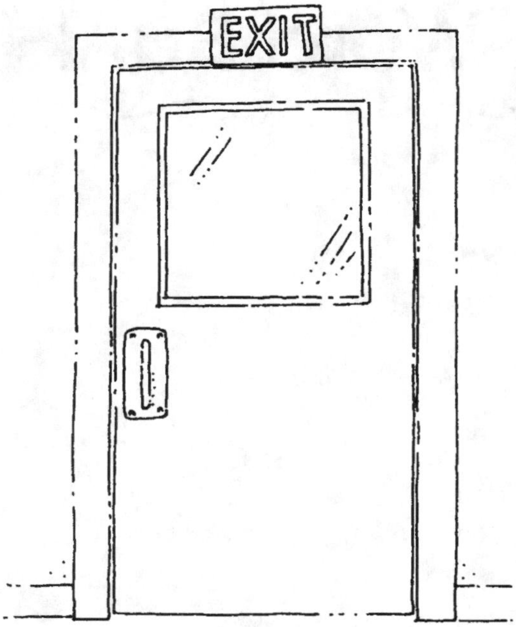

exit

yogurt

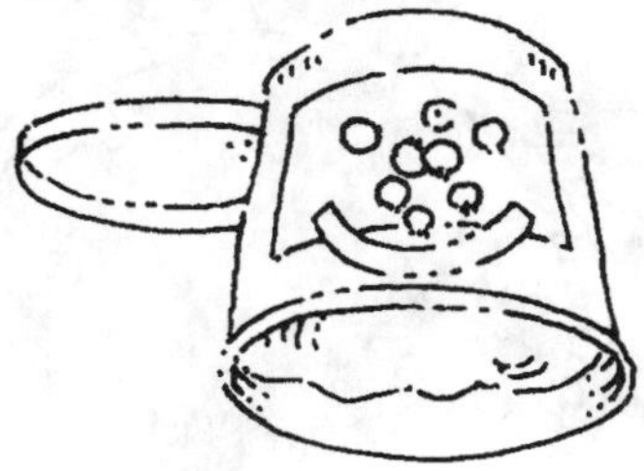

yarn

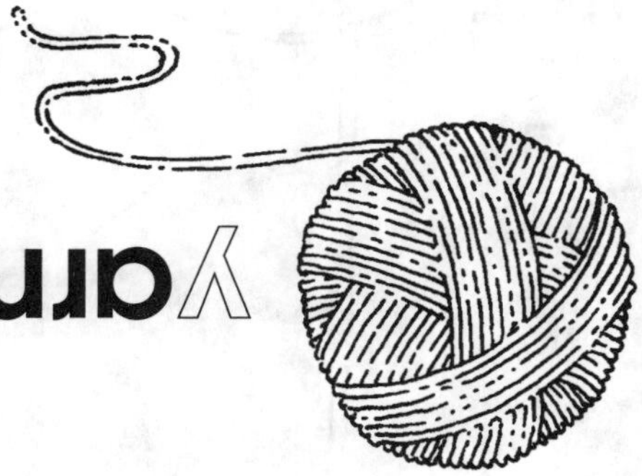

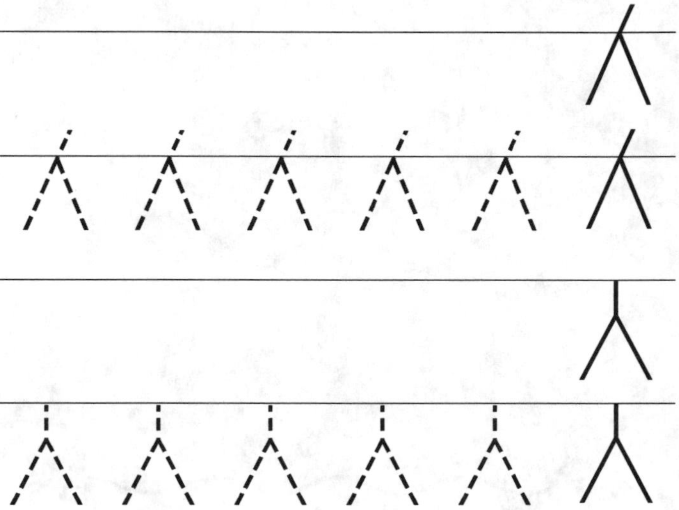

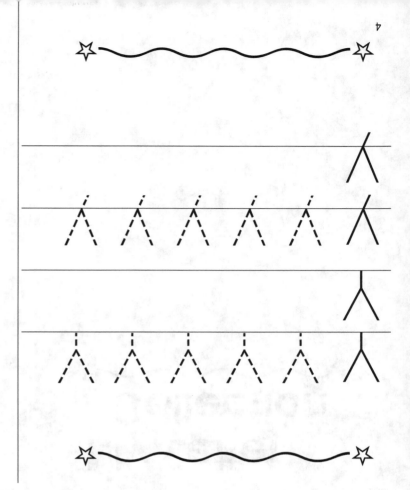

My Letter Yy Word Bank

______'s Letter Yy Book

My Letter Yy Collection

yo-yo

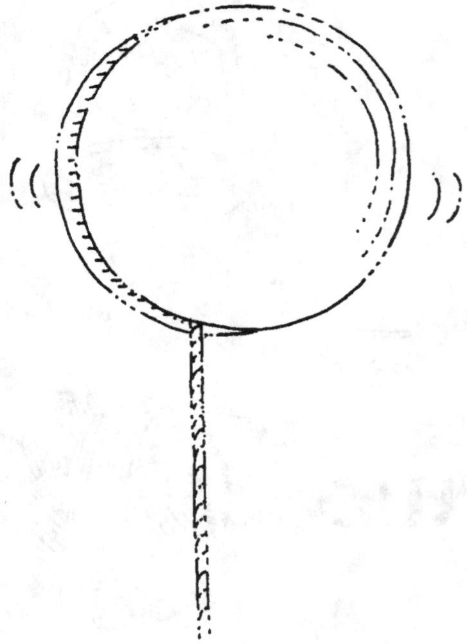

Letter Yy Collection

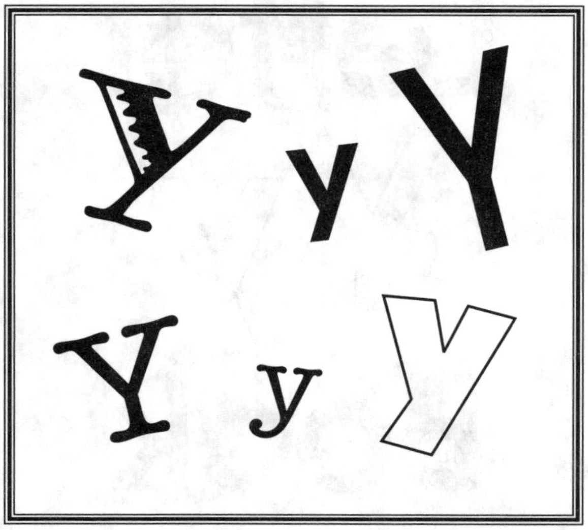

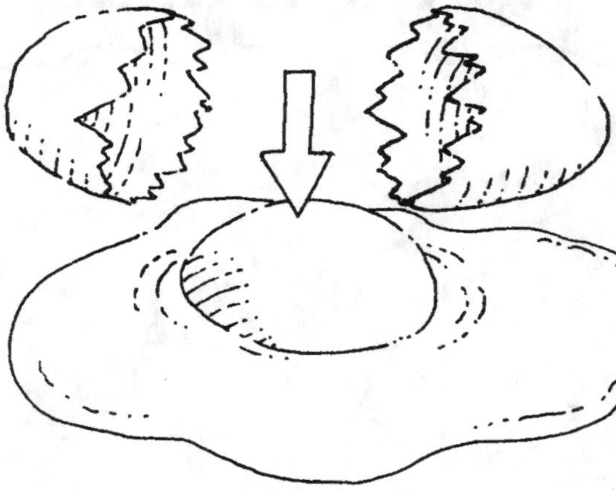

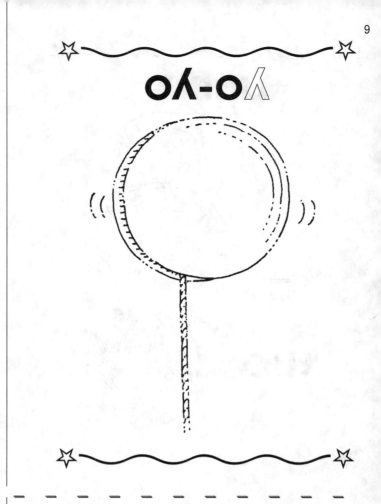

yolk

zebra

0

zero

Z Z Z Z Z Z

z z z z z z

My Letter Zz Word Bank

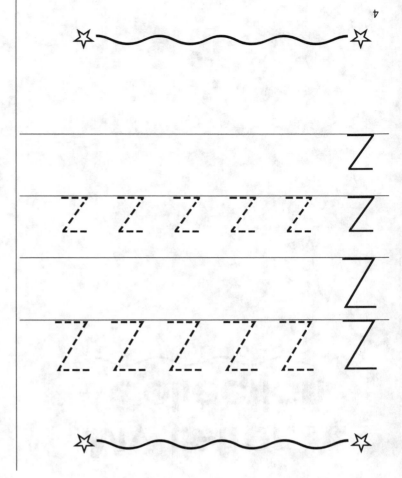

________'s Letter Zz Book

Letter Zz Collection

My Letter Zz Collection

zipper

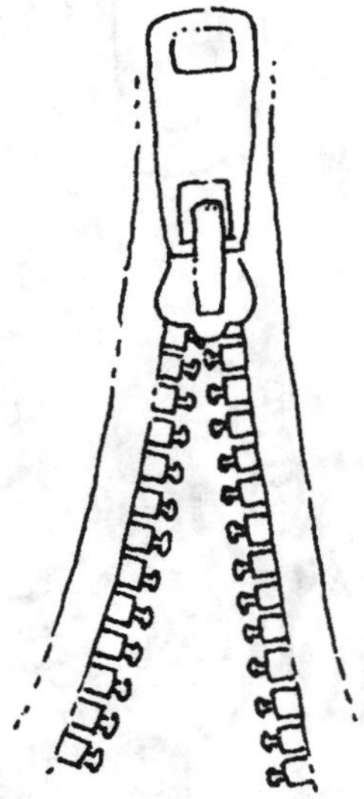

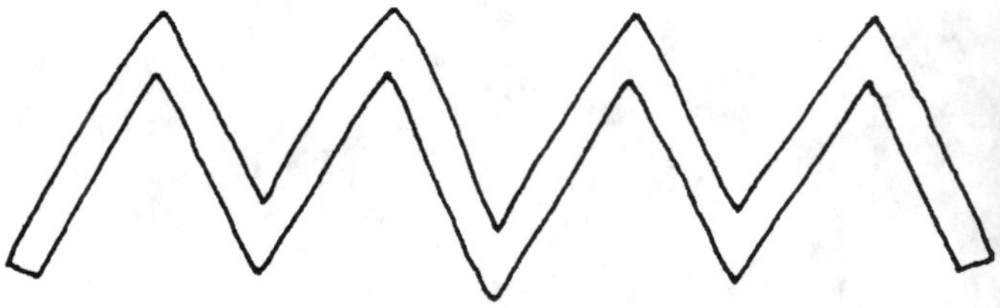

zigzag

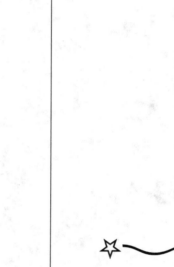